S0-BRR-472

Compassionate Living for Healing,
Wholeness & Harmony

ALSO BY JOANNE STEPANIAK:

Being Vegan
The Vegan Sourcebook
Vegan Deli
The Saucy Vegetarian
Delicious Food for a Healthy Heart
Vegan Vittles
Table for Two
The Nutritional Yeast Cookbook
The Uncheese Cookbook

Compassionate Living for Healing, Wholeness & Harmony

JOANNE STEPANIAK

To Michelle
With appreciation and love,
Joanne Stepaniak

KEATS PUBLISHING

LOS ANGELES

Library of Congress Cataloging-in-Publication Data

Stepaniak, Joanne, 1954–
    Compassionate living for healing, wholeness & harmony / JoanneStepaniak.
        p.   cm.
    Includes index.
    ISBN 0-658-01088-3
        1. Caring. 2. Conduct of life. 1. Title.
    BJ1475 .S84 2001
    170'.44—dc21

                                                                        00-067854

Published by Keats Publishing.
4255 West Touhy Avenue, Lincolnwood, Illinois 60712 U.S.A.

Copyright © 2001 by Joanne Stepaniak

All rights reserved. No part of this work may be reproduced, stored in a
retrieval system, or transmitted in any form or by any means electronic,
mechanical, photocopying, recording, or otherwise without prior permission
of the publisher.

Director of Publishing Services: Rena Copperman
Executive Editor: Peter Hoffman
Managing Editor: Jama Carter
Editor: Claudia L. McCowan
Project Editor: Judith Liggett
Text design: Laurie Young

Printed and bound in the United States of America

International Standard Book Number: 0-658-01088-3

01 02 03 04 05 VP 18 17 16 15 14 13 12 11 10 9 8 7 6 5 4 3 2 1

To the light within all.

Let it shine.

CONTENTS

INTRODUCTION

Compassion is an intrinsic and indispensable part of the human experience. Whether we are involved in endeavors that promote compassion—such as peace, social justice, human rights, animal rights, or religious or spiritual work—or if we simply want to become kinder and more loving people, compassion can benefit us personally by enriching all that we do and everyone with whom we come in contact.

Nearly all of us are familiar with compassion because it is something we customarily enjoy giving as well as receiving. Yet there is much more to compassion than most people discern, and there are many ways to expand its potential beyond our standard understanding of it as empathy toward others.

Our appreciation of compassion is deepened whenever it is missing from our lives. I have learned a lot about the need for compassion because I've had a great deal of experience not receiving it. Its absence made me brutally aware of a gaping hole in my life and my spirit. As a child, and even as a young adult, I had neither the words nor the acumen to express my longings or expose my anguish, yet the pain sliced me apart; it was alarmingly real. I have witnessed similar distress in others who had no support systems to cushion life's blows and no one to take delight in their successes. Being denied compassion made them furious at the world and at themselves because they felt they were unworthy of being loved. As a result, they often made reckless choices, lashed out at others, and grew mistrusting and resentful. Eventually their hurt and rage turned inward, transforming into self-doubt, loathing, and rejection.

Living without compassion is dangerous, for ourselves as individuals and for our world at large. It has taken me many years to comprehend how compassion—or rather, the lack of it—can destroy self-esteem and confidence. Through my work in counseling and mediation and the wisdom of several ancient philosophies, I have discovered how our private grief can be converted into brilliant illumination. This book is a compilation of the insights I have gained, spanning several decades of searching for and exploring the heart of compassion.

We all have had times when we've ached for others to hear us and to care, but no one was available, able, or willing to respond to our pleas, ease our pain, and love and accept us unconditionally. My personal and professional involvement with compassion has made me realize the potential that its presence holds and how valuable it is to those who receive it. No one has ever died from an overdose of compassion, but many believe that compassion undoubtedly saved them from certain doom. Indeed, compassion *can* work miracles. It is the secret ingredient to solving every disagreement and redeeming any relationship. In fact, we believe so strongly that compassion is the defining quality of being human that we created a specific word to reflect this notion: *humane.*

Being compassionate begins inside us, blooming from within and growing from the inside out. Benevolence always follows this progression. As we heal internally through self-directed love, we develop and strengthen our abilities to advance that love outwardly. When the intangible emotion of compassion touches a palpable, living being, it becomes activated and productive. It is at this juncture that the power of compassion is ignited and we achieve the ability to create peace within ourselves, nurture peace within others, foster harmony in the world, and reconcile with all the earth's inhabitants. This is the promise of engaged compassion, a point of hope and healing found only in one special place—your open and willing heart.

1

Foundations
of Compassion

Compassion is the emotion of empathy we feel toward individuals other than ourselves who are suffering. It allows us to identify with others' pain, from our own emotional histories, without personally experiencing what they are going through. Our firsthand knowledge of what it's like to suffer helps us to appreciate that another's hurt is similar to our own.

We cannot see pain; we can only identify it by its outward manifestations. Even when people tell us they are hurting and describe in graphic detail what they are feeling, there is no way for us to verify their claims. In good conscience, we must accept on faith that they are suffering despite our inability to confirm their pain directly.

Virtually all people are compassionate to one degree or another. A compassionate nature appears to be an innate, although not uniquely human, characteristic. It is observable even in young children and penetrates distinctions of culture, race, and ethnicity. Our recognition that others hurt as we do has led to social customs and mores that reflect this awareness. Although these may differ among countries, cultures, and ethnic groups, standards of courtesy and respect, which emanate from our sense of compassion, exist throughout the world.

THE POWER OF MIND

Because compassion is an emotion, it is passive. That is, although it can spur us to acts of kindness or prevent us from behaving cruelly, compassion, like all feelings, is basically inert. It rattles around inside our heads, but it doesn't have much of a life of its own outside our private musings. It also is invisible. As with pain, we cannot see, touch, or perceive another's compassion except when it is externally communicated through words, countenance, or behavior. As a result, compassion doesn't do anyone any good unless we are motivated to express it. Until compassion is activated, it remains relatively useless.

Activated compassion is *engaged compassion*. Only engaged compassion can provide help to suffering individuals, and only engaged compassion can have a promising effect on our lives and on the lives of those around us.

> Compassion doesn't do anyone any good unless we are motivated to express it.

All charitable acts are kindled inside our minds with thoughts of loving-kindness (tenderheartedness) and empathy. The more we contemplate the goodness in others, the more we are inspired to reach out and help them in the ways they want and need most. So although compassion may be provisionally dormant within the confines of our minds, our conscious acknowledgment of it is a necessary first step toward making it functional.

If we hope to induce favorable change in the world, we must first reflect the outlooks and demeanors we wish to see enacted. Knowing this is heartening because it means there is something each of us can do to improve social conditions and promote justice and harmony. We simply start with ourselves.

It is empowering to realize that the vast majority of problems we face originate within each of us and can be overcome in just the same way. Of course, we do not have control over many of our circumstances, but we do have the ability to master our responses to them. Our thoughts lead to attitudes, and our attitudes lead to action. According to a basic law of physics, all action creates change. Depending on the nature of our thoughts, our attitudes and hence our actions can have a positive or negative effect on ourselves and everyone and everything with which we come in contact.

THE PATH OF HEALING

Our modern world is restless and turbulent. We all want to feel safe and free, but when we seek answers outside of ourselves, we fail to tap into a source of strength and power that is with us all the time: our minds. When we heal the way we think—convert our damaging thought patterns into healthful ones—we will alter what we say and do. Each of us holds a key to mending our ailing world and restoring the harmony we crave. As the timeless adage asserts: Let there be peace on earth, and let it begin with me.

Engaged compassion incorporates a variety of philosophies and perspectives to draw the power of loving-kindness out from the realm of theory and into the practical world. It provides a sensible path that can guide us toward hope, serenity, and joy as we come to better understand ourselves and our places and purposes in the scheme of life.

> Each of us holds a key to mending our ailing world and restoring the harmony we crave.

The gift of engaged compassion is available to everyone. If we choose to receive it and agree to the responsibilities associated with it, we can realize wondrous transformations in ourselves. In addition, there is a ripple effect. Like the wind scattering seeds far and wide, our acts of loving-kindness radiate far beyond our earthly awareness. Thus, engaged compassion has an incredible capacity to create extensive positive change within our individual and collective bodies, minds, and spirits.

2

Investigating Our
Compassionate Nature

Most people are kind, considerate, and thoughtful and express their compassionate sides in a wide variety of ways. We are courteous to others, remember family members' birthdays and anniversaries, donate money to charity, do volunteer work, lend a hand to neighbors in need, and offer a listening ear to our friends. We exhibit compassion countless times in the course of an average day. Think about it for a minute, and try to recall all the compassionate acts you performed in just the last forty-eight hours. Write them down. It might surprise you how many deeds you've done that fall in the category of active compassion. Holding open a door for someone, allowing an elder to take your seat on the bus, smiling at the grocery store clerk, encouraging a colleague, comforting a child, forgiving your mate, or simply rolling with the punches demonstrate common, everyday benevolence that enriches our spirits and uplifts those around us.

Compassion is not a stranger. Even though we cannot see it, we can recognize its effects. When compassion is engaged, it is not only powerful, it is empowering. Just as a gentle rain can polish the craggy edges of a mountain over time, so can the delicate touch of compassion smooth the upheaval in our lives.

> When compassion is engaged, it is not only powerful, it is empowering.

Because you are already on the path of compassion, traveling further down the trail is a relatively straightforward task. You are on course, and your innate and experienced sense of compassion is a handy compass to help keep you there.

DIGGING DEEPER

If you currently engage your compassionate nature, why isn't what you already are doing sufficient? The answer is hard to pin down, partly because we each are unique in our experiences, but mainly because we share the perplexing challenge of examining our beliefs objectively. Trying to look at ourselves nonjudgmentally is like asking the image in the mirror what it sees.

Each of us wears a set of invisible cultural blinders that narrows our points of view and colors our perceptions. Few of us are even aware of our blinders because we have worn them all our lives and they simply seem to be part and parcel of who we are and how we regard the world. Nevertheless, these blinders perpetually filter what we observe, thus thwarting our abilities to consider life's full panorama or scrutinize with clarity what we do see.

Most of us have no idea that our perceptions are restricted or distorted in any way. What we choose to observe, how we interpret what we notice, and the opinions we hold dear are what we label as "reality" or "just the way things are." How we *experience* the world is the way we think it actually is—for everyone. We tend to get defensive about our perceptions because we trust that they are absolutely accurate.

The unique combination of our experiences, values, assumptions, and expectations about ourselves, others, and the world at large make up what are known as our *worldviews*. Our worldviews are reflected in the way we relate to our friends, acquaintances, and strangers, and how we react to the forces of nature and society.

A worldview consists of our beliefs about:

- what is—what is real (ontology)
- the relative merit and value of what is (axiology)
- how we and others ought to behave (ethics)
- how things that exist are ordered and related (logic)

No two worldviews are exactly alike, which makes our comprehension of life highly individualized. Because few of us detect anything askew with our worldviews, there is no compelling reason for us to question them. It would seem pointless, at least on the surface, to doubt what we assume to be "the truth."

7

Our ideas about what is "true" and "right" are shaped by family as well as ethnicity, subculture, race, religion, peers, and the culture at large. When new concepts mesh with our beliefs about the world, they penetrate and become part of the fabric of our worldviews. However, when new concepts clash with our current set of assumptions, they are typically filtered out of our worldviews and discarded as false.

Throughout our formative years, parents, family members, religious institutions, teachers, and other role models encourage us to be compassionate. But they also place limits on that compassion by deliberately suppressing ideas that challenge the worldviews they wish to instill. Consequently, as adults, our blinders interfere with our abilities to be compassionate to those outside the periphery of our emotional sights. We can't care about those whom we refuse to acknowledge; in fact, we don't even think about them. If, by chance, something out of the ordinary slips past our filters and into the fields of our emotional vision, we generally respond in one of the following ways:

1. pretending it doesn't exist,
2. ignoring it,
3. dismissing it as erroneous,
4. rationalizing its irrelevance,
5. fearfully driving it away, or
6. taking a closer look at it.

Based on these possibilities, worldviews can pressure people to do monstrous or heroic deeds. They precipitate bigotry, hatred, violence, and war. They can also be the impetus for social insurrection as well as a catalyst for moral evolution.

BROADENING THE HORIZON

People don't like to have their worldviews challenged because taking off our blinders is not a painless proposition. When we agree to consider ideas that contradict what we have always believed, we concede the possibility that we have been wrong all along. With such an admission comes a near-obligatory constraint to surrender our present viewpoints for dissimilar but "more correct" ones and, accordingly, submit to change. This can have a domino effect, because when we overhaul one of our belief systems, all our other assumptions get called into question, too.

It takes courageous and committed people to examine their worldviews, tear away their blinders, and pursue lives without illusion. Good or bad, right or wrong, our beliefs provide a haven of familiarity and comfort. They insulate us in much the same way a padded box provides protection for fragile objects. Nonetheless, when we push out the walls of the box, we find that instead of shattering from exposure we regain our freedom, sharpen our clarity, and expand the very core of who we are.

Anyone is capable of lowering these blinders; it only requires a longing to see the truth. But first we must acknowledge that our blinders exist. If we deny that we aren't seeing "the full picture," we are doomed to maintain our misconceptions and continue our present patterns of behavior. Steadfastly clinging to conventional ways of thinking causes us to become complacent and desensitized. Without remaining open to alternative points of view, we have no choice but to perpetuate the attitudes and actions that provoked our present disharmony.

Removing our blinders does not necessarily require cataclysmic changes in our lives. We are already compassionate, so

9

we're walking on well-trodden ground. But when we learn to see and think in fresh ways, we are able to expand the boundaries of our compassion, blaze trails, and explore footpaths previously unknown.

> Compassion, once activated, is the ultimate example of an endlessly renewable resource.

Despite our compassionate nature and the many kindnesses we bestow on others, most of us place limits on what we think is acceptable compassionate behavior. We calculate the appropriate time to dole out our compassion and carefully determine whom we think is deserving of it. It is compassion with reservation. We methodically ration our benevolence as if it were in limited supply. It is as though we believe we have only so much love to go around, so we better guard it cautiously. Fortunately, the opposite is true when it comes to humane caring. The more we extend our loving-kindness, the more of it we receive in return. Compassion, once activated, is the ultimate example of an endlessly renewable resource.

EXPLORING THE TERRITORY

Our worldviews convince us to draw parameters around compassion, relegating it to particular groups whom we deem worthy of our notice and concern. Visualize the rings that spread from a pebble when it is thrown into a pond. The closer to the pebble, the smaller the rings; the farther away from the pebble, the larger and more encompassing the rings. Our compassion is divided similarly, according to another's proximity and likeness to us.

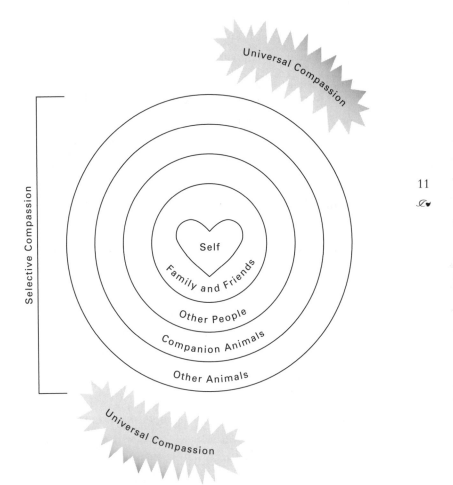

FIGURE 2.1   DEGREES OF COMPASSION

11

The pebble is at the center of all the rings. It represents each of us and the compassion we apply to ourselves. It is from this midpoint that all other forms of loving-kindness must grow. Understanding how to reach out to others begins with learning how to love and care about ourselves. Self-oriented compassion teaches us to respect our bodies and attend to our physical, intellectual, emotional, and spiritual needs. It fosters forgiveness, patience, and confidence. Like the unconditional love that parents extend to their children, self-oriented compassion bids us to love ourselves despite our presumed failings. Although self-directed compassion is a crucial element in cultivating empathy for others, being stuck at this level and not moving beyond it can lead to narcissism. Furthermore, people who are maladjusted at this level may be susceptible to engaging in antisocial behavior.

The first ring around the pebble is other-directed compassion, which encircles our families, close friends, spouses or partners, and children. These are people who are part of our emotional communities and are most like us. With this type of compassion, caring is reciprocal, mutually gratifying, flowing back and forth among members with little effort. It is easy to be compassionate toward those with whom we have much in common, because our worldviews coincide and we can readily relate to their feelings and beliefs.

The second ring outside the pebble is compassion for people who are similar to us but are outside our immediate realms. They may be kindred spirits or groups with whom we interact socially, know remotely, or have never met but with whom we feel a definite connection. Included here are people of our same religion, ethnicity, or subcultural group; people whose lifestyles or occupations correspond to ours; people who have endured the same tragedies or challenges that we have; or neighbors who live in close proximity.

This type of compassion can also extend to those we know little about but with whom we connect on an altruistic plane. At this level, for example, we grant compassion to the children of strangers, homeless people, oppressed groups, victims of crime, or victims of war or other crises—such as famine or natural disasters—in our own or other countries. Here we find that compassion is a more selfless but removed form of empathy founded on a detached sense of justice. Particular elements of our lives parallel certain other people's, so we can open to empathy based on what we have in common, even if it is just our mutual humanity.

As we move farther away from the pebble, the circles become large enough to provisionally embrace other species. With the third circle, we embark on the first level of interspecies empathy. This circle delineates compassion for nonhuman animals with whom we are close and have direct personal interaction, such as our companion dogs and cats. Through this one-on-one association, we discover that in spite of enormous differences that make it difficult to confirm each other's feelings and perceptions, we can learn to care for each other based on reciprocal affection and a common link of shared experiences.

The outermost ring of compassion is empathy for nonhuman animals with whom we have no direct contact and very little in common. It is akin to second-ring compassion in that it contains the element of altruism and there is no direct reciprocation. It, too, is based on a remote sense of justice, and, like

13

third-ring compassion, it is rooted in a concern for other living beings. However, people who apply fourth-ring compassion do not extend their mercy to *all* living beings. Their interests are directed only toward specific groups or species of animals that are designated arbitrarily as "important," "valuable," "endangered," or "in need of human assistance or intervention."

Collectively, these various circles, or degrees, are known as *selective compassion*. We can pick and choose among them, employing only those levels that appeal to us at any given time. With selective compassion we determine who warrants our concern based on a random hierarchy of value.

If we consider the rings in reverse, we can see how selective compassion could involve a pattern of discrimination. At the outermost rim we find compassion for those who are least like us. For many people, this stage of caring is superfluous because it is so far removed from their realms of experience that they are emotionally unable to connect with it. As we travel inward toward the pebble, where caring becomes more intimate and personalized, many more of us are willing to grant compassion to those with whom we feel closely aligned.

> As long as we maintain the position that certain lives are more important than others, we perpetuate disharmony and conflict.

This bias arises from the theory that "I matter and you don't." According to this premise, those who are most like us merit compassion, while those who are dissimilar to us do not.

Selective compassion necessitates a partisan point of view. It demands that we assess the value of every living entity in relation to what we perceive as our own worth. Consequently, selective compassion fosters intolerance, prejudice, and bigotry, and contributes to dissension and injustice.

As long as we maintain the position that certain lives are more important than others, we perpetuate disharmony and conflict. However, when we operate from the axiom that *all* life has value and is equally sacred, we nurture an atmosphere of serenity and respect.

This brings us to the final and most encompassing form of empathy, which is *universal compassion*. It includes compassion for all living beings, human and nonhuman, near or far, alike or different. It is the recognition that all sentient life is interconnected and that all our actions, both direct and indirect, affect the welfare and well-being of similar and dissimilar others. Universal compassion is impartial—it doesn't display favoritism, nor does it arrange a subjective order of empathy based on lesser or greater value. It consists of the pebble in the pond and all the rings surrounding it, as well as the air above it, the water around it, the basin beneath it, and the earth extending infinitely beyond. In other words, universal compassion embraces all living beings equally, including the earth that sustains us.

The image of the pebble and rings merely illustrates the expanse of empathic human emotions, which are, of course, intangible. Rarely is compassion as cut and dried as in this analogy. In reality, our demonstrations of loving-kindness are fluid because our empathies fluctuate both in range and capacity from day to day, moment to moment.

15

THE UNITY OF LIFE

Universal compassion is the essence of and impetus for engaged compassion. It is the gauge that measures our capabilities of achieving inner and outer harmony. It is also a guide for how to live with mindful awareness (thoughtful attentiveness to all that we think, say, and do) and is a reminder that our presence on this earth is shared with many others.

We are merely one piece of the puzzle that makes up life in the universe. Only when we recognize the unity of all life can we really feel at home in the world. We become fully human when we join with nature and embrace our animal family. Each creature, large and small, has its place and purpose in the scheme of things. Despite our differences, we are interdependent, and we share many similarities.

> Only when we recognize the unity of all life can we really feel at home in the world.

All living beings, human and nonhuman, hunger for sustenance, strive to avoid harm, tire with exertion, seek to be comfortable, and passionately attempt to stay alive. We breathe the same air, drink the same water, and live beneath the same vast sky. Each of us feels pain, and each will die. Each will leave its mark on the world in some unique way.

When we focus too narrowly on the small parts of the world we inhabit, we become overly involved with our personal losses and gains and ceaseless wants and desires. But when we remember the larger community of life and open our hearts to it, our own daily ups and downs lose some of their gravity. When we see the world as if through the eyes of others, we cannot help but grow in our compassion.

3

Releasing the
Bonds of Ego

Compassion is in many ways its own recompense. There is
an indescribable joy to be gleaned from performing acts
of kindness that cannot be found elsewhere, and this exhilaration often inspires people to continue or repeat charitable
behavior. Although the private cheer of benefactors is not the
purpose of engaged compassion, it is certainly a welcome
bonus. Nevertheless, our attachment to it can interfere with the
actual aim of giving.

This catch-22 is associated with every act of altruism.
When we participate in selfless service for the benefit of others,
it is true that we can obtain great personal satisfaction. However, if we engage our benevolence *for the purpose* of appeasing
our own desires, or even just to feel good about ourselves, we
undermine our efforts. When this occurs, selflessness turns into

selfishness. Our mind-sets become less about helping others and more about helping ourselves.

There is nothing fundamentally wrong about feeling gratified when extending kindness. It is a perfectly natural response to give ourselves a pat on the back now and then. But problems arise when we expect contentment, recognition, or appreciation from others in return for our consideration.

THE WAY OF PARADOX

If acts of compassion did not make us feel virtuous, nobody would do them. This is a principal fact about human nature. In general, we like to engage in activities that confirm our faith in our own basic goodness. Taken as an ancillary benefit, the joys we receive from giving are relatively benign, and, in moderation, they can even spur us forward in our benevolence. However, there is a point where this pleasure can become the sole driving force behind our behavior. It is then that any gains we might have achieved are lost.

When our egos become entangled with our efforts to help others, we are no longer providing selfless giving. Instead, we are giving to get, and that offsets any positive return we might attain. Our fulfillment becomes contingent on the rewards for our actions, and hence we place demands on the recipients of our good deeds. Whether we predict particular results, expect some sort of compensation, or want a show of gratitude, what begins as generosity turns into self-indulgence.

The same is true of performing acts of kindness just to feel righteous. In this case, good feelings elude us as we succumb to arrogance and pride. However, if we enlist engaged compassion because our hearts compel us to heed the suffering of others, and if we divorce ourselves from any potential personal gain, then the rewards can be many.

Whenever you engage your compassion, take precautions to guard your serenity and sidestep your ego. Here are five essential guidelines:

1. *The attitude you have about what you do has a greater bearing on the benefits you derive than does the aftermath of your endeavors.* Therefore you must be fully cognizant of your motivations throughout all phases of your undertakings.

2. *The effects of your generosity are relevant exclusively to the recipients.* Therefore you must release your emotional investment in the end result, whatever it may be.

3. *Giving is its own reward.* Therefore you must relinquish your interest in any personal gain and remove all stipulations you might place on the outcome.

4. *The beneficiaries of your kindness are your equals, not subordinates.* Therefore you must treat them with respect.

5. *There is much greater fulfillment in letting others shine than there is in attempting to overpower their glow with your own.* Therefore you must invite others into the spotlight as you graciously step into the shadows.

21

LETTING GO

The idea of giving freely with no strings attached is alien to many of us. Although most organized religions and spiritual philosophies celebrate the concept of charity, our capitalist system encourages us to assess worth in terms of dollar value and power. We are advised to ask the question, "But what's in it for *me?*" Therefore we are reluctant to enter into any arrangement unless the ends can justify the means and the outcome can be guaranteed to reap an advantage for us, even if that edge is only public admiration or private self-acclaim.

Broadly speaking, our culture subscribes to the notion that giving should be painless. If our contributions involve substantial self-sacrifice, we begin to wonder, "What's the point?" We laud philanthropists who have riches to spare and who won't feel a pinch if they donate a small amount of it to charity. Yet we rarely offer public acknowledgment of the sparse offerings from those with considerably less. This isn't to say that giving must devastate us in order for it to be worthwhile, but for engaged compassion to be personally meaningful, we must forfeit something of substance, be it money, time, comfort, or convenience. Without surrendering a palpable part of ourselves, the act of giving is rendered perfunctory and hollow.

THE WAY IN

Extricating our egos from this process of dynamic caring eliminates our fears of failure and disappointment. Because there is no self-serving investment, there is no reason to feel discouraged, angry, or shamed if our efforts fall through. If our hearts are loving and open, condemning others or ourselves is fundamentally impossible, even if we feel defeated. The cardinal motto of engaged compassion is simple: Do the most good and the least harm.

When we engage in universal compassion, we advance a philosophy of reverence for life. This is an indiscriminate and active ideology that requires our alert participation. If we are mindful of our thoughts, words, and deeds, we will bring to life a spirit of loving respect that can reach and affect everyone around us.

Just as your caring is reflected through your attitudes and actions, those in your midst will naturally respond to and mirror your manner and behavior. To test this theory, try the following exercise, called *The Healing Awareness of Smile:*

> First, center yourself and calm your mind. Sit comfortably in a straight-back chair, but don't sit all the way back. Place your feet flat on the floor, keep your back erect but relaxed, and rest your hands gently on your knees, palms down, or loosely cupped, palms up, on your lap. Close your eyes, release the tension from your face, and curve your lips into a half-smile. Breathe slowly in and out through your nose, keeping your exhalation slightly longer than your inhalation. With every out breath, feel your body becoming more and more relaxed as it sinks more deeply into the chair.
>
> Relax your abdomen and let it move easily outward as you inhale and naturally recede as you exhale. Do not force or try to control your breathing. Just lightly observe the air as it enters

23

and exits your nostrils—the coolness of air that is inhaled, and the warmth of the air that is exhaled. Keep your attention softly focused on following your breath. If your mind begins to wander, gently guide your concentration back to your breath. Let any thoughts drift past like clouds, without grasping at or clinging to them. Don't forget to retain your half-smile!

Now, still breathing through your nose in the same fashion, and still smiling, pause briefly after each inhalation and exhalation, retaining or suspending your breath for just a moment or two. Take ten to twenty slow, steady, not-too-deep breaths in this manner, pausing ever so briefly after each inhalation and each exhalation. When you are finished, relax your breath and breathe normally for another minute or two, eyes and mouth closed, until you are ready to stretch gently and stand up.

Keeping your half-smile and your peaceful center, go where you know there will be plenty of other people—the grocery store, the post office, the mall, or even a busy avenue or park. Make sure you keep your half-smile intact as you travel to your destination. Once there, look for opportunities to extend a bit of kindness. Keep your heart open and avoid analyzing what you see. Remember to maintain your half-smile!

The kindness you offer may be as simple as a warm, larger smile to other shoppers, a sincere "thank you" to the store clerk, retrieving an object someone absently dropped, pulling an item from a shelf that somebody cannot reach, giving directions, opening a door, or just greeting those you pass with your smile or a friendly "hello." Observe the reactions you get without critiquing them.

How did this exercise make you feel? Did anyone smile back at you? Did people appear pleased or cheered when you assisted them? Did you notice anyone's demeanor brighten just by your smiling presence? Did anything unusual happen? Is doing something like this out of the ordinary for you? Overall, how do you think you affected those around you?

You might consider this exercise simplistic, but that is just the point. Engaged compassion doesn't require us to be or do anything extraordinary. All those seemingly mundane or trifling deeds of thoughtfulness add up and can make a big difference to others. We don't need to travel halfway around the globe or donate all our time and money to charitable organizations in order to be actively compassionate. There is much we can do right in our own small corners of the world. If we look for opportunities to be compassionate, we will find them, regardless of how large or small we deem them to be.

25

> The cardinal motto of engaged compassion is simple: Do the most good and the least harm.

You already possess the basic know-how and skills to expand peace and harmony in yourself and in the world. What remains to be determined is your strategy. One method is to assign yourself a comprehensive list of compassionate acts to perform each day, week, or month. Another simpler and perhaps more practical route is to just go about your routine activities with greater awareness and intention to do good. Either way you can contribute significantly to a more serene and caring world. Your presence *does* matter. If you are willing to take these crucial forward steps, you can favorably influence your environment in ways that might exceed your highest hopes. Just imagine what bliss would unfold if everyone everywhere decided to do the same!

MOVING TOWARD PEACE

26
♔

When you selflessly engage your compassionate nature, you benefit in profound ways, both inwardly and outwardly. Inwardly, you know that you are making conscious choices to do what you believe is honorable and right. By being mindfully and dynamically compassionate, you open the door to feeling good about who you are in ways that would otherwise be inaccessible to you. It is spiritually and emotionally uplifting to seek out occasions to demonstrate compassion. Just being attentive to how you think, speak, and act can trigger a comforting and liberating sense of inner peace.

The outward advantages to engaging compassion are striking. Your actions may not necessarily affect others in any preconceived or obvious ways, but a positive and generous outlook is infectious. Whether or not you impress others visibly, what you think and how you behave definitely affect your own mood and spirit. Knowing that your manner of living conforms with your highest ideals invites serenity of conscience. Inner turmoil is eliminated because there is no conflict among what you believe, what you think, what you say, and what you do. This inward peacefulness is then mirrored in all your outward actions.

The effects of a calm demeanor combined with acts of loving-kindness leave a subtle, lingering trail wherever you go. It invites other people to follow your example, to walk the path of compassion, and to participate in mindful giving according to their own individual styles. We may never learn how or even whether our benevolence touches the hearts of others. Nonetheless, engaged compassion summons us to have faith and know that our intent to do the most good and the least harm— irrespective of the outcome—is our only moral avenue and our only hope for a just and humane world.

27

LIVING IN THE MOMENT

In each moment, we have the chance to do good, do harm, or do nothing. This means you can change not only your disposition and conduct, but the very course of your life at any time you choose. The only obstacle that ever really stands in your way is your attitude.

Engaged compassion must be reborn every moment in order for us to realize its potency. When we are regularly attentive to the life around us—people, animals, insects, plants, and the earth herself—we can intuitively recognize when we should reach out, intervene, hold back, or just observe. Simply by paying attention, we can catch opportunities to engage compassion before they pass us by.

> In each moment, we have the chance to do
> good, do harm, or do nothing.

When we attend to every moment, we empower ourselves to eradicate, or at least reduce, many of the stressors of modern life. Each moment becomes full because we are present in it. Being present means being awake, and being awake means being alive. Accordingly, we cannot be fully alive if we are worrying about or appraising the past, our flaws, our problems, someone else's deficiencies, or what might happen in the future.

Being here, now, in the immediacy of the moment allows you to avoid the pitfalls of guilt, while responding compassionately in every moment grants you the potential to live without regret. Given any particular set of circumstances, if you are mindfully aware, you will know that you have done your best. Certainly, it is inevitable that on occasion your judgment will fall short, you will make poor choices, or you will hurt someone unintentionally. This is an inescapable part of being human. Engaging compassion is not about grasping at some unobtainable level of perfection. There is no question that we will fumble; it is simply a matter of when. Still, it is not enough to know about and prepare ourselves for the worst. Compassion is concerned with how we own up to and take responsibility for our mistakes and whether we are mature enough to admit our failures and rectify our wrongdoings.

All conscionable people experience remorse when they are thoughtless or cruel. Your conscience speaks to you in a still, small voice, reminding you to acknowledge where you were remiss, urging you to offer heartfelt apologies, and advising you to remedy the situation quickly. There is a great power to heal in an honest apology, especially when accompanied by a pledge to never repeat the offending behavior. If no redress is possible, then it is vital to bring your awareness back to the moment at hand; otherwise you will become preoccupied with worry and self-recrimination, thereby losing command of the present.

When we are fully immersed in the immediate moment, there is no room for hindsight or foresight. When you find yourself veering off in one direction or the other, a gentle reminder is all that is needed to bring yourself back to the here and now. There is no need to chastise yourself for slipping away from the moment at hand. It is virtually unavoidable, and chiding your wandering mind will only divert your attention once again. It takes practice and a concerted effort to learn how to remain present. Training the mind is analogous to exercising the body: discipline, hard work, and abundant motivation are the not-so-secret ingredients.

The benefits of this type of mind work are not only an increased capacity for awareness, relief from countless causes of tension, and enhanced potential to activate compassion. It also gives you a chance to enjoy your life more completely because your mind is wholly engaged and focused where your body is—where it can only be—the present. A common method used to stay in the moment is to bring your attention to your breath. All you need to do is lightly observe your inhalations and exhalations—their length, speed, and quality of the flow—without trying to regulate them. Here are three approaches you can use (employ only one at any given time):

29

1. Follow your breath's path as it enters and exits your body, expanding and deflating your lungs.
2. Concentrate on drawing in the air surrounding you and then releasing your breath back into the universe.
3. Focus on the tip of your nostrils where the cool air comes in and warm air comes out.

Another simple technique to draw your mind back to the moment is to mentally note each step of every activity you perform. For instance, when you are sitting and are getting ready to stand, silently think, "I am transferring my weight to my feet. I am pushing my body up from the chair with my hands on the armrests. I am straightening my legs and standing upright." If you are taking something out of the cupboard, silently think, "I am opening the cupboard door. I am reaching for the box of crackers. I am placing the crackers on the counter. I am closing the cupboard door."

Noticing and mentally logging your activities serves several purposes:

- It obliges you to slow down and pay attention to the moment at hand.
- It makes you fully conscious of all that you say and do.
- It forces you to think before you speak or act.
- It minimizes misunderstandings and hurtful behavior.
- It improves your memory.

OPENING TO POSITIVE ENERGY

There are two principal external benefits that engaged compassion can inspire: vitality and glow. Vitality is the physical vibrancy we derive from reducing inner turmoil. Our thoughts and outlooks have a dramatic effect on our physical well-being and can be determining factors in whether we become sick, how debilitating an illness will be for us, and how rapidly we recover. Whatever steps we take to reduce anxiety and increase tranquility will only prove beneficial for our health. By eliminating conflicts of conscience, focusing on the present, and developing a loving approach to life, engaged compassion eliminates the stresses and fears that can contribute to illness. Concurrently, engaged compassion nourishes our emotional centers, which sustain us, heal us, and fuel our will to live.

What you think and believe reaches far beyond your own mind and body. Not only do your attitudes cause you to do helpful or harmful deeds, they can affect others even before you speak or act. We've all known someone who exudes charm or charisma and lights up a room just by entering it. We've also met people who make us squirm and cause the hairs on the back of our necks to stand on end whenever they're within earshot. Whether we call it good vibes and bad vibes, magnetism and aversion, or simple intuition, it is an unmistakable reaction we've all experienced time and time again.

Although not deliberately, each of us emits a powerful force-field that precedes us and charges those around us. It is this mental electricity that attracts or repels others and allows them to see your true nature despite what you might do to try to conceal it. You cannot prevent this energy from being released. Nonetheless, you have the ability to temper it and transform other people's impressions of you simply by modifying your perspectives.

Unlike other therapeutic modalities, engaged compassion relieves us of the burden of our egos. This is because it accents that which exists outside of us. When we learn how to release

31

our grip on pride and vanity and attune to truths much larger than ourselves, we will automatically become less self-centered and develop greater tolerance for and acceptance of our own limitations and those of others.

As you expand your compassionate nature, your inward-flowing energy will be altered as profoundly as your outpouring positive energy. Eventually, your inner calm will shine through you like sunlight through sheer curtains, and you will develop a perceptible glow. Others will be drawn to you because they will feel welcome and safe in your company. Your unspoken tenderness will herald the presence of a trusting, gentle spirit, and your devotion will captivate those around you.

32

There is only one way to control the release of the energy we exude, and that is by converting it from within. Vitality is cast by a sound body. A loving heart takes the form of glow.

PERSONAL RESPONSIBILITY

Cutting through the shackles of ego does not mean ignoring our own needs or living vicariously through the comfort and good cheer we bring to others. Quite the contrary. Engaged compassion embraces the significance of *all* life—our own included! Thus it advocates that we take good care of our emotional needs and physical health, get sufficient rest, exercise regularly, eat a healthful and harm-free diet, cultivate supportive and nurturing relationships, and nourish our spirits through creative outlets and joyful experiences. Furthermore, it opposes deleterious activities and unwholesome, abusive, or addictive behaviors that could hurt us or others or cloud our minds and prevent us from making sound decisions.

Accepting our place in the scheme of life does not make our value greater or lesser than anyone else's. We are each responsible for and answerable to ourselves. But we are also accountable to each other and to the family of life of which we are a part. We can no more separate ourselves from the whole of existence any more than we can separate the cells that constitute our bodies. Therefore we need to strike a balance between other-directed and self-directed concerns and learn how to recognize when one ought to take priority and when both can and should be addressed simultaneously.

4

Living Without Struggle

Opening our hearts to compassion allows us to experience the whole of life, to discover truth, and to behold the beautiful and unsightly with equal regard. Living in the moment, an essential aspect of compassionate practice, helps us to realize and accept the impermanence of all existence. Joy invariably gives way to sadness and then winds its way back to joy again. Flowers bloom and wither, becoming mulch for the buds of spring. Seasons turn and return. Like waves, our emotions, our bodies, our relationships, our worldly possessions, and all living entities are constantly ending and becoming, dying and being reborn.

> The only truth we can be assured of in life is that nothing will stay the same.

It may seem unfair or unfortunate that things cannot remain what they are or have ceased to be what they once were. But if we cling to them and try to prevent them from changing or departing, we will continually heap suffering on ourselves. The only truth we are assured of in life is that nothing will stay the same. Taking this revelation to heart will save us, and others, a lot of needless anguish. It can help us loosen our grip a little, because no matter how tightly we clasp what we hold dear— life, love, beauty, happiness, beliefs, or our corporeal existence— they will inevitably fade.

Mindful awareness that we and everything we treasure are not only constantly transforming but will eventually perish and pass away can help us better appreciate the frailty of all life— human and nonhuman—and empathize with the sorrows of others. Every living being is intrinsically connected in this way. We all fear for our own demise and must cope with and adapt to the unavoidable insecurities of life. Knowing that we are alive together, right now, sharing the same canopy of sky, the same earthly resources, and the same instinctual yearning to survive, is a powerful and bonding realization.

Impermanence can in many ways be consoling because it doesn't only affect the people, animals, and things we cherish. What we don't like is temporary, too. This means that our pain, suffering, angst, heartaches, and bad moods will ebb and flow right along with our joys. Conceding the temporality of exis-tence makes hard times a little easier to bear and good times ever more precious. It also can make us more forgiving and tolerant of what we consider to be shortcomings in ourselves and other people.

BEING TEACHER

All human beings have an inherent potential to function as informal mentors. We are all teachers, whether or not we provide obvious or direct instruction or even choose to function in this capacity. Wherever we go we affect those with whom we interact, leaving behind bits and pieces of ourselves that remain long after we depart. Our attitudes and demeanors reverberate independently of our control, creating an invisible imprint in our wake.

If we are mindful of all that we think, say, and do, our marks will be constructive. If we operate in a fog and disregard the needs of others, we can be hurtful or damaging. Often we are unaware that others are learning anything from what may seem to us to be just our customary behaviors. Typically we go about our business quite oblivious to any outside scrutiny. Nonetheless, our smallest acts of consideration, rancor, or disregard can deeply move someone else. The tone of your voice, the tilt of your head, your eye contact, nervous gestures, and the way you stand and carry yourself make just as significant an impression as what you say, perhaps speaking volumes more. Words can be deceptive, but body language betrays our innermost secrets and divulges our real feelings.

If we profess one thing but do the reverse, we teach mistrust. If we offer kindness when it is unexpected, we teach thoughtfulness. If we are brusque and vulgar, we teach disrespect. If we are patient and gentle, we teach consideration. If we are cold and detached, we teach indifference. If we extend mercy and benevolence, we teach compassion.

Regardless of age, intelligence, education, or experience (ours or theirs), others learn from us, so it is prudent to pay attention to the lessons we proffer if we want them to be helpful, not harmful. Spend some time every day to consider what it is that others might be learning from you. Often what we *presume* we are teaching is not actually what we *are* teaching, and the lessons learned may very well be the antithesis of our original intentions. When we bellow at others, are we guiding them in courtesy and respect or coaching them in guilt and blame? When we chastise, are we enlightening about forgiveness and mercy or teaching condemnation and shame? When we belittle or humiliate, are we demonstrating grace or exemplifying revenge?

> Only through living our convictions and teaching by example can we make progress toward peace and compassion.

Each association with another individual—young or old, healthy or incapacitated, kind or cruel—is an opportunity to personify and extend the compassion that we would like to receive and see manifested in the world. Only through living our convictions and teaching by example can we make progress toward peace and compassion. Even if our endeavors do not appear to reap results, we can never fully know the influence we are having. Our attempts alone foster personal tranquility, if nothing else. Because this sense of serenity promotes our overall well-being, it augments and reinforces all of our peaceful efforts by contributing to a general spirit of loving-kindness.

BEING STUDENT

There are periods in our lives when many of us claim to know it all or insist we have little left to learn. In which case, the suggestion that we should be students again may seem a bit off-putting or demeaning. Nonetheless, assimilating new information and ideas is not age- or experience-related. We can maintain the learning process and grow both intellectually and emotionally throughout our lives, if we so choose. Learning is a sign that our minds are as alive and vibrant as our bodies. Indeed, the ability to learn ceases only when our brains and hearts stop functioning. If we choose to stop learning, our minds are as good as dead.

Despite our ability to absorb information, much of the time we function as if we are in a daze. We might see clearly enough to go about our normal routines and keep from bumping into people or objects, but few of us actually stop to study and digest our surroundings, our emotions, or our feelings moment by moment. Typically we are overwhelmed with too many ostensibly pressing activities to pause and fathom what it's like to really be alive. Before we know it, our days seem numbered, and we're left wondering where all the time has gone.

39

> The ability to learn ceases only when our brains and hearts stop functioning. If we choose to stop learning, our minds are as good as dead.

Often it takes a tragedy or shock of some proportion to jolt us back to reality, if only briefly. The death of a loved one, a near-fatal accident, or the discovery of a life-threatening illness frequently jars us enough to awaken our sleeping minds. In these instances we are more apt to realign our priorities because trauma is one of the few times they naturally fall into place. It is ironic that when our lives crumble out of control, we can become more lucid and rational. Major disturbances force us to come to terms with what is most important in our lives, and they push us to find the means and motivation necessary to make crucial changes.

Fortunately, we don't have to wait for a catastrophe to have the sensation of being fully alive. Living deliberately and with conscious awareness is within the reach of all of us all the time. In fact, these elements are essential to becoming compassionately engaged because we can't provide dynamic empathy if we aren't paying close enough attention to know when it's needed and what to do.

40

> The best teachers realize how much their students have to teach them.

At the same time we are teachers, we are also students. Certainly the best teachers are those who realize how much their students have to teach them. For many of us, it is hard to admit that we don't have all the answers. Our jobs, families, and even our self-esteem may cause us to feel that we need to be in constant control, so letting down our guard a bit to allow new ideas to stream in or to grant someone else a chance to be "right" or take the lead can be frightening.

Sticking to worn-out assumptions and refusing to surrender what we want to believe is "correct," despite internal confirmation to the contrary, can whirl us in the precise opposite direction from where we want to go. The more we grit our teeth, clench our fists, and mutter under our breath, the more out of control we actually appear and become. Strongly desiring to be "right" in the face of those who disagree only makes us angry, and it will probably make our opponents angry too, or, at the very least, unwilling to hear what we have to say. What it won't do is convince them we *are* "right." The only way to win anyone over is simply not to try. Like it or not, it's really the only chance there is of preserving consonance.

When we rigidly cleave to a position, we construct a shell around ourselves that disconnects us from others. This contributes to a sense of isolation and sabotages our compassion by making us feel estranged from, instead of a part of, the whole. Letting go of our need to always be right or have the last word helps to keep us unobstructed and spacious inside. By doing so, instead of losing ourselves in the enormity of the universe, we will actually feel more grounded, complete, and self-aware.

If we maintain a willingness to learn, others will be freer with us because they will sense that we are accessible and accepting. Openness creates an atmosphere of mutual respect, give and take, in which both parties are more likely to listen to each other than demand to be in control. When we submit to being students, we don't relinquish our authority; we rise above it. Just as significantly, we may come to accept new "truths" and alternate points of view that can enrich us in remarkable and unexpected ways.

41

When we submit to being students, we don't relinquish our authority; we rise above it.

Being a student means learning to think with the openness of a child—a neophyte, a beginner—and to disregard preconceived notions. If our spaces for learning are filled with presumptuousness and arrogance, there will be no room left for gleaning fresh ideas and our minds will stagnate and petrify. Maintaining the soft heart of a student, on the other hand, creates a flourishing mind that can keep us youthful, invigorated, interesting, and interested in life.

Accepting your role as student is in no way a coercion to accept perspectives other than your own. Instead, it is an invitation to explore and examine other standpoints and consider whether they ring truer for you than those to which you presently subscribe. Ultimately, "truth" is a subjective designation, and it is much more flexible and far less static than we generally like to admit.

The suppleness of our minds and the expanse of our hearts are directly correlated with our zeal for being a student. Although we alternate this role with being a teacher, both are equally important and consequential. If we commit to only one —teacher or student—we cut in half our opportunities to understand and grow in our compassion.

42

PROGRESSING THROUGH ADVERSITY

It is not necessary to try to be a model teacher or a flawless student. At the core of your being, where your heart resides, you are perfect and omniscient even now. Engaged compassion does not aim for any particular ideal except to peel away the superficial layers of our external lives that prevent us from experiencing the truth we already possess inside. Its purpose is to alleviate suffering—our own and others'—through awareness and conscious living. The more we are attentive, the greater the probability that we will stay open and sensitive to the heartaches in our midst and can allow the shields and masks we hide behind to dissolve.

Despite its ability to allay suffering, engaged compassion is not a panacea. When we open to loving-kindness, we yield to the raw, ordinary, and spectacular twists of life with equal intensity. Gazing into the face of misery is heartrending and certainly not for the squeamish or weak of spirit. When we allow another's pain to touch our tender spots, we can become profoundly haunted. This may be excruciating and frustrating, particularly if there is not much we can do to abate the problem.

Deciding to live with awareness does have its downside. Truth is uncompromising in its honesty and does not spare our feelings. When our views are unobstructed, all aspects of life— from the depressing to the uplifting—come into clearer focus. Hence, in order to fully savor life's splendors, we must be willing to witness its hideous parts as well.

43

This is not as ominous nor as difficult as it may sound at first. Primarily, our fears are born of the unknown. Most of us are unaccustomed to confronting the seamier sides of life and so, initially at least, they may loom large. Yet if we turn and bolt, mentally or physically, we attempt to flee not only the realities of suffering but our fears of them. No matter how far we run or how deeply we bury our heads, truth will not disappear. Once we have observed it, the only escape is to dust off our blinders, cover our eyes, and numb ourselves.

Because our worldviews cause so many of us to live in states of perpetual denial, we not only skirt many painful aspects of life, we miss much of its abundant beauty and joy, too. Avoiding truth—whether positive or negative—keeps us walking an endless tightrope, continuously filled with dread over the prospect of falling, because we know that if we do, nothing will ever be the same.

FINDING BALANCE

For most of us, our equilibrium seems dependent on safeguarding our worldviews. Shaking things up—or rattling the high wire, so to speak—disrupts our patterns and throws our mindsets completely off kilter. Engaged compassion puts such a kink in our routines. This is perhaps why so many otherwise kind people choose to draw a line in the sand and suppress their circles of compassion. It is simply safer, more convenient, and less unsettling for them to maintain the status quo.

Yet putting conditions on the extent of our compassion restricts us personally as much as it limits our ability to evoke goodwill around us. Even though we might desire to uphold our current views and habits, in the long run we will shortchange ourselves and everyone else in the process. Turning away, averting truth, does nothing to eradicate our own or others' suffering.

There is a happy medium, however, between selfless zealotry and sanctimonious resistance to change. Seeking this parity—the nucleus of inner peace—is one of the most fascinating aspects of practicing engaged compassion. Discovering "right reason" helps us make "right choices" so we can ultimately find the "right way" and distinguish where our energies are best spent moment by moment.

There are a limited number of hours in a day, and each of us can be spread only so thin. Consequently, it's tempting to succumb to guilt about "not doing enough" or fall prey to the inverse, reactionary self-indulgence. Guilt can urge us forward and inspire us to do more than we thought we were capable of, but it can also hamper us with remorse. We are already compassionate and good enough. Engaged compassion is not designed to change the essential nature of who we are but to deepen our experience of it. It does not measure the quantity or quality of what we do. Its sole objective is to reduce suffering through mindful awareness and conscious living.

> Engaged compassion is not designed to change the essential nature of who we are but to deepen our experience of it.

45

Because there are no finite goals to strive for, there is no basis for self-reproach. Our observance of truth—at this moment —is sufficient. It alone will call forth the wisdom that already dwells within us.

Taking care of ourselves and letting bliss into our lives demonstrate the personal side of compassion. Joy and content-ment are the essential counterweights that stabilize other-directed energy. Opening to and accepting our inner experiences are the precursors to giving openness and acceptance to others. Without recognizing and attending to our own basic needs, our efforts will be lopsided, and eventually they will cause us to become cynical, resentful, and bitter.

Engaged compassion teaches us to follow the middle path, the one that winds between narcissism and asceticism, extravagance and prohibition. It is the way of moderation—the golden road to balance and tranquility.

5

The Four Branches of Engaged Compassion

The four branches of compassion can be compared to the four prime directions that are indicated on a compass, and, like a compass, they can help us find our way. No branch is superior to another; all are equally important on the continuum of engaged compassion. These branches operate concurrently within us and are interdependent. Each is a vital component of a whole human being.

Throughout your life you have ready access to these four branches, even though at times they may elude your awareness or seem inert. You may discover that you are drawn to one or more of them and are utterly disinterested in others. Consequently, it could be tempting to ignore the branches you don't care about and devote your energy and attention to those that are more compelling. All the same, without parity among the branches, your trunk of compassion is doomed to be unstable and lopsided. Eventually it will become completely asymmetrical, making it very difficult to properly right it again.

The sooner you address all four branches of compassion, the more rapidly you can plumb the full depths of your benevolent nature. At any given moment you can activate a branch's potential just by drawing your attention to it and acknowledging its presence. Observe how all four branches are (or are not) represented in your awareness and your daily activities, and practice maintaining equilibrium among them.

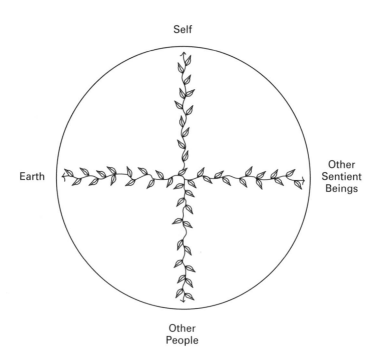

FIGURE 5.1   THE FOUR BRANCHES OF COMPASSION

THE BRANCH OF SELF

Broadly speaking, we are a mass of contradictions, especially when it comes to cherishing ourselves. We seek solace in every external remedy, from material abundance to excesses in food, drink, and other temporal pleasures. Then, when we discover their detriments or are shamed by our behaviors, we look for consolation by equally overindulging in austerity, abstinence, or atonement, until we feel so deprived we begin the cycle all over again.

As a culture, we celebrate the accumulation of possessions and monetary wealth while simultaneously extolling philanthropy. We praise humanitarian endeavors but crave lives of leisure and self-gratification. We long for freedom but dodge responsibility. We yearn for tranquility but are fearful of boredom. We decry slavery and murder but advocate incarceration and capital punishment and routinely impound and massacre innocent animals. We aspire to peace but we glorify war. It is no wonder we are puzzled and unable to sort out our priorities!

All equanimity begins in our minds and is expressed initially by how we treat ourselves. Most people think that compassion is what we give to others and that to dote on oneself is extravagant. This encourages self-sacrifice at the cost of our health and sanity and contributes to martyrdom, neither of which leads to happiness or inner peace. When we believe that taking time out for ourselves and attending to our needs is indulgent, we are destined to feel contrite whenever we do.

Taking care of ourselves is not a luxury. It is a necessity and the launchpad for all other forms of compassion. Personal attentiveness is not the same as selfishness, so feeling ashamed about accommodating our needs is unwarranted. Overindulging at the expense of our own or others' well-being, however, is a different story. Nevertheless, it is a rare circumstance that calls for sacrificing one duty over another. In general, we are easily able to fulfill our personal obligations to meet our own needs while still lending kindness and mercy to those around us.

Cherishing ourselves encompasses caring for our physical, emotional, intellectual, and spiritual health. When one or more of these areas is overlooked, all are diminished, and we become imbalanced and incapable of functioning optimally. In addition, paying attention to and heeding our own very real needs helps us better understand and empathize with the needs of others.

Principles of Physical Well-Being

Taking care of your body is crucial because your body houses your spirit—that inexplicable spark we call "life." Without a healthy body we are unable to operate freely, and we become dependent on others to assist us. Furthermore, when we are ailing, our focus is redirected to our discomforts, making it difficult to concentrate on anything else. Infirmity can be exhausting—mentally, emotionally, physically, and financially—so you owe it to yourself and to those close to you to take every reasonable measure to avoid it. Once your health has been compromised, it is taxing to reclaim it. This may seem like just plain common sense, and it is, but too often we ignore our bodies because we think they are immune to illness, or will rebound as they did in our youth, or we reason that we are just too busy with more pressing tasks to take the time to attend to them.

There are, of course, certain factors that influence health over which we have no control. But there are countless things we do that undermine our well-being and set up a conducive environment in which illness can develop. Here are five indispensable strategies to integrate into your daily routine to safeguard your physical health.

1. Get sufficient rest; spend time each day doing nothing.

Listen to your body's call to sleep, nap, or take a break from activity. Go to bed at a reasonable hour and arise before or at dawn, making sure you get at least seven or eight hours or more of sleep each night. Allow yourself periods of downtime during the day—planned intervals when nothing is scheduled and there are no demands on you. Although this may sound inconceivable, if you believe that a respite is restorative and vital, you will ensure that it takes precedence. When rest is made a priority, we can somehow find the time for the five- or ten-minute breaks we need throughout the day to do nothing else but relax.

2. Engage in a healthful amount of suitable activity.

Your body is an amazing machine that needs to move in order to stay fit. Set aside twenty to thirty minutes every day for stretching, walking, bicycling, swimming, yoga, or tai chi to keep it in peak condition. It is harder to get a body into shape than it is to keep it in shape once it's there. Make movement and exercise an enjoyable part of your daily routine, and you won't have to give it much more thought. If necessary, arise a half hour earlier than usual. First thing in the morning is one of the best times to exercise; then you won't have to be concerned about it the rest of the day. An alternative is to use your lunch break to go for a walk, or you can do a few stretches or yoga asanas (postures) while dinner is in the oven. However you do it and whichever form you choose, find some space in your schedule

51

for exercise. It is an essential part of caring for ourselves and therefore a key component of engaged compassion.

3. Eat a proper diet.

A compassionate diet is one that is based on living foods, not remnants of suffering and death. It is perhaps the height of hypocrisy to consume the objects of our compassion or to make arbitrary distinctions among sentient life forms in order to justify eating them. Center your meals around wholesome, health-supporting, plant-based foods, including whole grains, beans, vegetables, fruits, nuts, and seeds. You will feel healthier physically and, since you will not be compromising your ethics or sense of compassion, you will feel cleaner and stronger in spirit as well.

4. Pursue a right livelihood.

Engaged compassion necessitates that we do not perform acts of cruelty, fraud, or deceit toward other people or in any way exploit animals or the earth in the course of pursuing our occupations. Moreover, in addition to doing work that is innocuous, it is imperative to engage in efforts that help make the world a more loving and compassionate home for all. Appraise what you do for a living. If it is damaging to other people, animals, or the earth in any way, it is also destructive to you.

5. Conduct yourself ethically.

Because your body is the temple of your spirit, engaged compassion compels you to cherish and respect it no less than you do all other life. Participating in activities that are harmful to our bodies is the antithesis of active compassion. Therefore, promiscuous or unsafe sexual activity, violent behavior, gluttony, indolence, reckless driving, alcohol and drug abuse, or any other enterprise that puts our bodies in jeopardy conflicts with the principles of engaged compassion and should be eschewed by those who seek to fully practice them.

Principles of Emotional Well-Being

All suffering begins with our reactions to the circumstances in which we find ourselves. Because the mind is the seat of all emotional disturbances, when we learn how to respond to situations in ways that are not harmful to ourselves or others, we can retain emotional balance in spite of the challenges we face. When our emotions are unsteady, our physical health is put in peril, but this is not just due to foolhardy choices induced by impaired judgment. Under intense or extreme emotion—such as depression, fear, animosity, or anger—the brain triggers the release of potent chemicals into the bloodstream. With repeated or extended emotional flare-ups, these chemicals become toxic and can weaken the immune system, establishing a favorable environment for disease. In addition, emotional upsets impair our ability to think clearly and experience joy, thereby affecting all other realms within the branch of self-compassion.

Mastering our emotions requires more understanding than it does discipline. Acknowledging, observing, and befriending our emotions lets us mollify and transform them and move beyond the agitated states that keep us uncomfortably stuck. Employing the following five strategies should allow you to do just that.

53

1. *Practice self-acceptance.*

Within each of us there are attributes we admire, tolerate, or just plain deplore. Generally our assessments are based on subjective comparisons to what we believe we should be like, even though these fanciful ideals may have no foundation in reality. For most of us, when it comes to self-evaluation, it is painfully difficult to be objective. Although we may be quick to conclude what we dislike about ourselves, it is hard to take such harsh analyses to heart. When self-deprecating emotions surface, our initial reaction is to push them away. However, if we can befriend them and see them for what they really are, not what we *think* they are, we can gain many useful insights, including learning how to transform them into productive tools for personal growth.

Whenever you become embroiled in self-directed fault-finding, use the following exercises to help make the experience fruitful rather than destructive:

- Instead of turning away from your emotions, take a closer look at them, identify them, and try to name them. For instance, some common emotions we experience when we find fault with ourselves are fear, worry, anger, shame, frustration, disappointment, hopelessness, disgust, and remorse.

- Examine your emotions carefully, without criticizing yourself for having them. Hold them in your heart with gentleness and care, as if attending to a small and needy child.

- Notice how it feels to dislike parts of yourself. What are the physical sensations that accompany these emotions?

54

Observing how your feelings manifest in your mind and body validates their existence. Once they are acknowledged, they are no longer a threat and will lose their power over you. If ignored, however, they will flourish and dominate your thoughts in an unrelenting attempt to gain your attention.

At this moment you can be no different than you are. In the light of this moment, you are perfect—not in contrast to a fantasy prototype but in relation to all the world. Each living being is perfect unto itself, for there are no others like it. Cherishing who we are, inconsequential faults and all, is indispensable if we are to feel compassion for ourselves and anyone else. If we are incapable of accepting our shortcomings the same as we do our strengths, we will be unable to ever fully embrace others without similarly judging them.

2. Relinquish ego.

Emotional balance necessitates walking the line between selfishness and radical asceticism. If we recognize that we are part of all that is living and all that is living is a part of us, then there is no need to triumph over others. We can feel good about and satisfied with who we are without resorting to self-aggrandizement or belittling others in order to elevate ourselves. You do not have to blow out anyone else's candle for yours to shine.

In all our activities and relationships we must investigate whether our motives are genuine and pure, or whether we are driven by pride, arrogance, conceit, or self-doubt. Looking at each thought and situation honestly will save us, and others, significant pain. Admitting when ego is taking control deflates its hold on us and frees us from its inevitable repercussions—envy, contempt, and resentment. Releasing our attachment to ego

55

does not diminish who we are. Instead, the capacity to be humble exposes a quiet inner strength that generates greater self-esteem and outward respect.

3. Surrender outcome.

When we invest emotional energy in the consequences of our actions, we lose touch with the present moment and end up living in and for the future. We also set ourselves up for certain disappointment, because rarely do our hopes and expectations meet reality. To stave off frustration and the anguish of being let down, focus on what you are doing right now, instead of worrying about how it will turn out or what will happen next. This will allow you to do the best you can with what is directly in front of you. As a result, the chance of a positive outcome is greatly enhanced, even without dwelling on what it likely will be.

4. Remain present.

Irrespective of what we did in the distant past, completed a few minutes ago, or what we hope to accomplish down the road, this moment is all we have and all we can be assured of ever having. By reminding ourselves to stay present, we can prevent our experiences from eluding us and can gain the most from our lives. This means living *in* the moment rather than *for* the moment. Directing (or redirecting) our attention to the here and now shields us from disillusionment, curtails our grief from perceived past failures and injustices, and eliminates the inescapable frustration over our inability to control the future. The only power we have is now—and now—and now. If we are not awake in the present moment, we are not fully alive, physically, emotionally, intellectually, or spiritually.

5. Align priorities.

Coming to terms with what is meaningful to you is vital for your emotional well-being. So often we put vast amounts of energy into thoughts and activities that in the final analysis are relatively unimportant to us. We fret about issues over which we have no control, worry about imagined phenomena in the future, get all worked up over perceived wrongdoings, and sulk about the past. The emotions instigated by our thoughts are very real, even if the matters we are contemplating are long past or merely fabrications of our wandering minds. Our bodies react to them as if they were happening now, signaling the release of potent chemicals into the bloodstream, chemicals designed to activate the fight or flight response. However, when feelings are summoned by our thoughts and not by events taking place in the immediate present, fighting or fleeing serves no purpose. The chemicals remain lodged in our bodies with no escape. Over time, the persistent release of these chemicals can work against us, causing chronic states of anxiety, insecurity, anger, agitation, bitterness, resentment, cynicism, or fear.

Recognizing that your mind is the source of your emotional well-being and hence your overall health can help put your thoughts into proper perspective. Dwelling on the past and future, abstract and theoretical, is counterproductive and potentially very damaging. The following three pointers can help you keep your priorities in order and your mind firmly planted in the present:

1. Pay attention to your thoughts and notice when they are meandering or luring your mind in vain, judgmental, or destructive directions.

2. Acknowledge that what you are pondering is insignificant or irrelevant to you at this moment, and redirect your concentration to what you are doing and what is in front of you right now.

3. Be aware that all disruptive thoughts are generated by the urge to be distracted.

Minimize diversions by consciously and regularly pulling your attention back to the present moment. With this technique, you can, in due time, drastically reduce the detrimental effects of negative emotions and greatly increase your happiness. Aligning priorities is merely a matter of establishing constructive habits.

58

Principles of Intellectual Well-Being

Most of us know that our bodies and emotions can become imbalanced and that both need tender nurturing in order to stay fit. We rarely consider the health of the intellect, however, perhaps because we are less conscious of it. Generally we assume that learning is simply an integral part of who we are, so it's hard to imagine our intellect as a separate entity.

Actually, all the elements that comprise the "self" are interdependent. In our day-to-day functioning, their boundaries blend, so it is virtually impossible to ascertain clear distinctions among them. Even so, each principle can be isolated by its capabilities and primary function. In the case of the intellect, its purpose is to feed the mind information. Based on the kind and complexity of the information we receive, our minds process responses that are filtered and expressed through the other elements that make up who we are.

The information we assimilate can influence us positively or negatively. Therefore, it is critical to choose with care what we feed our minds.

1. Pick and choose.

What we allow to enter our minds colors and transforms our thoughts and attitudes. What we devote our attentions to determines what we observe. What we observe determines what we perceive. What we perceive determines what we think. What we think determines what we do. What we do determines what we devote our attentions to. It is an endless cycle that always begins and ends with our awareness.

It may seem that we have no control over what our minds take in, but indeed we do. If we want to desensitize ourselves, we seek matter or activities that steer our minds into a void. We may believe that such diversions give our minds a breather, but what they really do is steal them away by anesthetizing us to the moment. During some activities it is impossible to remain present and still be fully engrossed. For instance, watching a stirring movie, attending a rock concert, or reading a scintillating novel all require us to surrender to an illusion; our lives are purposely put "on hold." Where is the intellect during our participation in these diversions? Our bodies are involved, at least to a certain extent, and our emotions become entangled and heightened, but where do our conscious minds go when we engage in extraneous preoccupations? And, if they are still attuned, exactly what information are they absorbing?

There is a difference between escapist pursuits and art, film, theater, music, and literature that are illuminating, cathartic, thought provoking, challenging, or healing. Outlets that are

59

carefully chosen can furnish a context for intellectual stimulation and provide a common language with which to express our shared experiences. Instead of atrophying the intellect, such activities provide the perfect cerebral exercises.

You can screen what your mind consumes by prudently selecting what you attend to. If you are enraged to no constructive end by modern politics, avoid reading or hearing about them. If the study of botany uplifts you, learn more about it. If violent television programs disturb you, refrain from watching them. If observing the natural world exhilarates and revitalizes you, allot time every day to pay attention to it.

Although our minds are not blank slates, they can respond as if they were when we do not deliberately focus them. In addition, everything we take in has profound repercussions on our emotional, physical, and spiritual well-being. To fully engage your compassion, be aware of when you use distractions as an escape from your life and learn to guide your attention with discretion, knowing it is always under your command.

2. Stop to listen.

Our world is filled with beautiful, calming, inspiring music, if only we would take the time to hear it. Crooning birds, rustling leaves, the whir of insects, booming thunder, whispering winds, the patter of rain, and gurgling creeks constantly surround and serenade us with their harmonies. Sadly, our fast-paced lives, rapid transportation systems, and ever-expanding technologies drown out the music of the natural world, replacing it with a hypnotic buzz that pervades so furtively and monotonously we barely notice its presence.

Background noises such as the constant droning of television, radio chatter, and piped-in Muzak further prevent us from hearing our own thoughts and fully paying attention to our experiences. Their clamor fills our minds with random information, sometimes without our even being cognizant of it. These diversions may fleetingly entertain us, but they don't satisfy our deeper hungers. The more we tune them in, the less contented we become, and the more we find ourselves isolated from nature's soothing melodies and the hush of our own inner calm.

To attune yourself to the imperturbable world that exists perpetually within and around you:

- Make conscious choices about what you listen to.
- Hearken to the voices of nature and to the voice within your own heart.
- Keep outside distractions to a minimum, so you can actually hear what you are thinking and can relax in the serenity of a still and quiet mind.

3. Develop mental flexibility.

We generally associate agility with the physical body, not the intellect. But our cognitive abilities can also become stagnant and dull if not given proper, regular workouts. When we do not expose ourselves to fresh ideas and stimulating points of view, our minds become stale and unyielding. Then we are unable to pursue or recognize truth because we believe we already know all there is to learn.

When our minds are resistant, our thoughts become rigid, our attitudes grow stubborn, our demeanors turn obstinate, and our faces appear dour and tight. This is readily observable in

61

elders who have harbored anger, fear, or deep regrets about their past. Their bitterness becomes etched in their stiffened bodies and puckered expressions. However, if we study their joyful and vibrant counterparts, we find that people who appear the happiest are those who remain cognitively open and delight in challenging their intellect regardless of their age or ability. The bodies of these people look much more pliant and their faces and voices seem more gentle, bright, and receptive.

To develop or maintain mental flexibility, seek out media that connect you with the present and awaken your mind and spirit. Read enlightening books and magazines; watch informative films and videos; listen to instructional audiotapes; immerse yourself in the arts and humanities; or attend classes, seminars, workshops, and lectures that are mentally stimulating and cultivate inner understanding. Never stop exercising your intellect in this manner. By doing so, you will always remain agile, alert, and spacious.

4. Avoid mental overload.
Despite how hard we may try, it is impossible to know absolutely everything. Even though we persuade ourselves that we must study, read, and learn as much as we can, for most of us our mental capacities will always have their limitations. We can retain only so many facts and figures and, because so much of what we take in is completely inconsequential to our lives, a large part of it is rapidly forgotten. Moreover, pursuing unnecessary information can be like candy or a drug, a way to escape reality by engaging in an activity that is socially acceptable but nonetheless distracting and psychologically addictive. For instance, we might believe we are obliged to watch televised newscasts each evening

because we feel compelled to stay abreast of the latest events. What we see and hear might upset us, aggravate us, or cause us to become hardened and numb. How does this affect us night after night? Even if we can't recall the details of each report, the emotions they launch stay stuck within our minds, where they will continue to influence us long after the programs have aired.

If we respond to information in ways that are detrimental or if we use our intellect for diversion, it is perhaps far better to remain uninformed. We do not need to know all there is to know. It isn't practical or wise to even try such a senseless and vain feat. Going to the well, realizing that our buckets may come up empty, is humbling as well as enlightening. When we accept that we don't have all the answers—or sometimes any of them— we foster humility, grace, and intellectual receptivity.

Whatever we know is always shifting, morphing, coming and going. Knowledge by its very nature is not firm. Only the unknown is unchanging. Putting our faith in the unknown rather than the known is the path to resolute truth. It is also our only promise to stand on solid ground.

5. Create mental space.

In our modern-day pursuit of the greatest amount of knowledge in the least amount of time, many of us, at some point, experience information overload—a period of being utterly overwhelmed and mentally exhausted. At these times it feels as if there is absolutely no room left in our brains for even one more shred of information. In desperation and out of necessity, we shut down and block out everything that isn't essential.

You can thwart these chronic implosions by creating internal space for your mind to breathe and expand. This is most

63

readily accomplished through regular daily meditation. Any style of structured meditation will suffice—seated, moving (such as yoga, tai chi, or walking meditation), or contemplation with sound (such as chanting). All forms of meditation soothe and relax the mind and provide a gentle respite that can diminish or eliminate the desperation that comes from internal and external pressures. Furthermore, meditation enhances the practice of all aspects of engaged compassion, including all the principles inherent to the branch of self.

The centering and calming portion of *The Healing Awareness of Smile* exercise on page 23, is a simple but suitable meditation with which to begin. Start by practicing it once or twice a day for five to fifteen minutes at a time. Be dedicated and persistent. Approach your meditation with an open heart and mind and without expectation. Meditation is an excellent discipline to train in surrendering outcome. Do not give up if you do not notice results. The rewards of meditation are very subtle but also cumulative. They vary from person to person and even from day to day.

Principles of Spiritual Well-Being

The spirit is perhaps one of the most elusive elements of "self." Because it is intangible and forever transforming, it is hard to pin down its features and modes of expression. Still, if we look closely, we can see its imprint on all that we do.

The spirit is best defined as "life energy"—the force within each of us that prompts us to arise each day, allows us to be charmed by a budding flower or frolicking puppy, and inspires us to sing out with joy, cry out in woe, and be passionate about life. Our spirits cause us to feel animated and motivate us to overcome obstacles or illness to remain alive.

We feel most spiritually charged when we are engaged in activities that make full use of our natural gifts. All sentient life experiences similar spiritual awakenings, even though our aptitudes may differ. Just watch a dog chase after a ball or leap in the air to catch a stick, and you will see its spirit in bloom. Observe a hawk in flight, a cat's graceful vault, a horse galloping, or a child learning to walk. Each displays a special spark, a reveling in just being alive. These are the silhouettes of their spirits.

The spirit within us is enriched and amplified when the physical, emotional, and intellectual talents with which we are gifted are well utilized. When one area is damaged or neglected, our spirit suffers in turn, and our verve for life is diminished. Our spirits mirror how adequately or inadequately we are functioning in the branch of self and can help pinpoint the areas that need extra attention and nurturing.

One technique to restore or energize your spirit is to connect with the natural world on a regular basis. An easy means to do this is to take a stroll in the woods, a tree-lined park, or a garden in bloom, and drink in the wonders that abound. Notice the tiny insects, the scars and rivers in tree bark, the intricacies and miracles hidden in flower blossoms and leaves. Feel the grass and soil beneath your feet, the fragrant air against your skin, and the warmth of the sun. Touch the earth with your hands, and then reach for the sky. Feel your body as it moves and balances against its weight and the forces of gravity. Watch as your spirit stirs and swells within you. Feel it flowing, billowing, and coursing

65

through every cell until your entire being is flooded with élan and awash in a surge of life.

This exhilaration, this sense of aliveness, is the energy of your spirit. Like all the other principles of the branch of self, your spirit needs proper nourishment, rest, exercise, and attention in order to thrive. It flourishes when its sibling principles are healthy and working in harmony, and it, too, benefits greatly from the harbor of daily meditation.

THE BRANCH OF OTHER PEOPLE

Compassion originates from the point of self, but does not become fully actuated until its embrace includes those outside of ourselves. Engaged compassion begins with the familiar (our families and friends) and spreads to those who are similar to us in ways that are meaningful to us (such as race, ethnicity, religion, gender, occupation, economic group, and so forth). Because we readily relate to our families and friends on a variety of levels, share so much in common, have an ongoing personal relationship, and, for the most part, genuinely like each other, caring about and reaching out to them is usually second nature. In addition, these relationships are reciprocal—we give and receive, receive and give. It is through this requited emotion that we feel loved and are able to learn compassion for ourselves and for others. People who have not developed these close relationships early in life are often stymied in their ability to be compassionate, probably because they are still desperately in need of being loved themselves.

> Compassion originates from the point of self, but does not become fully actuated until its embrace includes those outside of ourselves.

Only after we master empathy for those with whom we have something in common can we broaden our compassion to include people dissimilar to us. This is the most difficult aspect of human-to-human compassion because it is easy to dismiss the suffering of others with whom we can't or choose not to connect. Indeed, there are times when we might think it is actually more convenient *not* to be compassionate toward those outside of our "inner circle."

Throughout history, humans have invented imaginary barriers that estrange them from certain groups of people whom they want to exploit. Whether it is war, racism, sexism, or other forms of brutality and discrimination, we malign those we want to manipulate in order to justify our cruel desires. We disparage groups of people by cursing them, devising epithets, and creating malevolent stereotypes that associate negative qualities with real or imagined characteristics. By distancing others in this way, we absolve ourselves of the guilt we have from taking advantage of them.

But humans don't stop at impugning groups; we denigrate individuals as well. We do it—consciously or unconsciously—because we are accustomed to assessing other people through the lens of our limited worldviews. Although we may not give it

much heed, we all regularly judge people by such random criteria as gender, skin color, age, sexual orientation, vocation,
income, accent, disabilities, height, weight, communication skills,
style of dress, general attractiveness, hygiene, grooming, and
mannerisms, among many others. Each time we make assumptions and pinpoint an "offensive" trait about someone, we desensitize ourselves to them and dehumanize them little by little.
Eventually we make them so repugnant that we become completely detached from and deadened to their feelings and needs.
Separating ourselves emotionally from particular people opens
the door to rationalizing our "right" to abuse them.

Every time we demean someone—even if it's only in our
own minds or through confidences to a friend—we damage ourselves and destroy a piece of our own humanity. Furthermore, we
wound the people we put down, perhaps in ways we cannot see
and will never fully understand. As a result, they may go on to
injure others in a haphazard attempt to restore their self-esteem
and reclaim their dignity, perpetuating a cycle of combustible
hurt and anger that can spread like wildfire.

The only way to heal ourselves of intolerance is to acknowledge it when it arises within us. When we look our biases straight
on and embrace them nonjudgmentally as a very real part of who
we are, we give ourselves a chance to understand their source and
in time transform and overcome them. Having prejudices does
not make anyone a bad person. Denying prejudices, on the other
hand, can make even highly principled people do incredibly horrible things.

Examining where our views are narrow and distorted promotes truthfulness within ourselves, our relationships, and our

interactions with people similar and dissimilar to us. There is no shortcut, however. Self-honesty is achieved exclusively through consistent practice. By consciously observing our physical and emotional responses to various groups of people, we can condition ourselves to not disregard our prejudices. When we pay attention to them, we can scrutinize and accept them for exactly what they are. Engaging our hearts of compassion obligates us to remain open and sympathetic toward all individuals and groups—despite how objectionable or irritating we may find them—no less than we wish to be accepted and regarded ourselves.

> Having prejudices does not make anyone a bad person. Denying prejudices, on the other hand, can make even highly principled people do horrible things.

69

THE BRANCH OF
OTHER SENTIENT BEINGS

There is a popular saying: Human beings aren't the only species on earth; we just act like we are. This maxim holds an incredible amount of truth and ought to be a clarion call to anyone on the path of compassion.

Too often we neglect or harm other life forms with glib justifications such as, "Humans are more important than animals," or "Animals were put here for our use," or "Animals don't feel pain," or "They were raised for a particular function, so it's okay," or "Their purpose is to serve us, so they don't mind." When erroneous opinions are presented as fact by the very individuals who stand to benefit most from them, humane people need to question their validity. There is no moral or scientific rationale to support the notion that animals do not feel pain or were created for an express function or to serve humanity. All life has meaning and value unto itself and a purpose and destiny independent of ours, even if we don't understand or appreciate it.

Stock excuses have been used throughout history to defend the subjugation of specific groups of people based on race, skin color, gender, age, and other superfluous qualities. As the combined consciousness of human beings has expanded, many of us have come to realize the perversion of such self-serving, unilateral thinking. In order to fully engage our compassion, the same must become true of how we view other animals and life forms.

When we label animals for utilitarian purposes—food, clothing, possessions, or tools—we steal their membership in the community of life, converting living, feeling beings into inanimate commodities. We have become so accustomed to the sight of dismembered corpses in a morgue, such as the modern supermarket, that we are not only no longer shocked, we are oblivious. As a whole, human beings will be unable to attain peace at any level as long as we condone the abuse and slaughter of animals, consume them, and use our bodies as their tombs. How could it be otherwise? It is irrelevant whether we participate in the killing directly, if we do nothing to protest or stop it and continue to subsidize it through our purchases and habits. Allowing others to do our "dirty work" does not absolve us of culpability. Thus buying meat, leather, or any other form of animal flesh, skin, bone, and appendages is akin to murder for hire.

Regardless of how fervently we champion the presumed "need" for animal consumption or disavow our parts in this ceaseless holocaust, the emotional repercussions from our roles are absorbed into our individual and collective psyches. We are a nation of assassins, whether or not we choose to admit it. Unless our systematic, routine exploitation and slaying of animals for food, fashion, education, research, entertainment, or any other purpose is confronted, acknowledged, and renounced, serenity will elude us. To achieve peace among people or nations, or recover our own inner peace, we must first make peace with the other species that share our earthly home. Until we do, tranquility will remain a stranger, because it is impossible to assuage guilt while continuing to engage in the same deplorable acts for which we seek clemency. We cannot create harmony in the world without initially finding serenity within, and that will not happen until the hurt and killing stop.

71

For many of us on the road of compassion, eliminating animal products from our diets and lifestyles seems like an unnecessary burden. Our hearts have turned to stone over this issue primarily due to our personal desires to maintain a way of life that indulges our complacency toward other species. Ignoring this matter, however, does not remove its blot on our spirits. Moreover, when we consume products of suffering and death, we ingest the residual energies and toxins that were discharged into the animals' systems, precipitated by their terror and pain, and that became lodged in their tissues when they died.

We cannot dismiss the frightening possibility that these forces have powerful and detrimental effects—psychically, emotionally, spiritually, and physically—on people who eat such decay.

There is plenty of room in our hearts to demonstrate compassion for ourselves, other people, and other animals simultaneously. We would be remiss to think that compassion is finite or that we need to dole it out methodically by taking a little away from one in order to give it to another. Just as parents can love all their children equally but uniquely, so can we engage our compassion toward all sentient life. To do anything less limits our natural capacities, stunts our inner growth, and deprives us of personal and universal peace.

72

THE BRANCH OF EARTH

The branch of earth comprises all the animate and inanimate life and organic substances that exist within or on her surfaces, waterways, and atmosphere. It may be hard to envision the earth as a living being, but she is no less alive and breathing than are we.

You and I are made up of billions of separate but interdependent cells and organisms that create the aggregate entities known as "you" and "me." All the various parts of our bodies operate in unison, each doing its own special task to keep us healthy. When one part malfunctions, even temporarily, we can feel lousy all over. But with excessive or prolonged problems, our bodies deteriorate irreparably and, eventually, they fail us.

In the very same way, the earth is our living body and we are just one of the many organisms that have taken up residence here. Even though this might make us feel small and insignificant, each of us plays a vital role in keeping our host vigorous and well. The earth sustains and nourishes us, just as it supports all life. It supplies an abundance of everything that is essential for animals and plants to survive and thrive. What is particularly amazing is how in this process all life on earth is interconnected. Not only do we share the basic resources that the earth provides, but we are part of an elaborate and well-balanced scheme. For example, mammals must breathe oxygen in order to stay alive. When we exhale we release carbon dioxide from our lungs. Plants absorb carbon dioxide through their leaves, and they release precious oxygen into the atmosphere. In essence, we are breathing in unison with the trees and plants. Every inhalation and every exhalation is shared by other life forms with whom we are interdependent.

73

The earth is no less alive and breathing than are we.

Much is unknown about the earth and the intricacies of her functions. We do know, however, that the soundness of her systems reflects her ability to sustain life. Countless species have perished since human beings first began ravaging the earth's surface, fouling her air, polluting her waterways, and attempting to control her delicate, intricate patterns. To be whole in our convictions, all seekers of compassion and peace must also be advocates for and active stewards of the earth. As with any act of compassion, we must protect the earth, not for ourselves but for all life and the body that is earth herself. In doing so, wholeheartedly and self-lessly, we will concurrently safeguard the interests of our own species and all those with whom we are mutually reliant. Taking care of the earth means, in part, making responsible consumer choices. Here are just some of the ways you can incorporate concern for the earth into your daily life:

- Limit consumption to what you truly need.
- Choose sustainably produced products.
- Minimize refuse.
- Recycle what you can.
- Buy recycled goods.
- Look for ways to reuse materials whenever possible.
- Utilize the least polluting transportation methods.
- Reduce energy use.
- Purchase organic food.
- Support small industry.
- Discourage new land development.
- Endorse building renewal and restoration.

In our day-to-day activities, there are numerous opportunities to make decisions that will affect the earth positively or negatively. It is our responsibility to always select the wisest and soundest options. As ambassadors of compassion for the earth's community, we simply have no other alternative.

6

Gateways to
Engaged Compassion

In order to bring compassion to life, we must pledge to make it a consistent and dynamic part of all that we do. Thus the first step in activating compassion is to become aware of our daily practices, including our thoughts, our attitudes, and how we treat ourselves and others. Most of us are deeply entrenched in routines that make us apathetic without our even being aware of it. We don't stop to scrutinize our lives because we often feel we have so little control over them. This assumption stems from our seeing the world as a towering, elaborate hodgepodge and ourselves as tiny, helpless specks. When we retract the wide-angle lens and zoom in closer to home, we discover that we always have significant command over the most critical and influential elements of our lives—our minds, our manners of being, and our behaviors.

Nonjudgmental self-observation is the most direct route for overcoming indifference and bringing habituated conduct to light. Just by noticing what we are doing and examining our patterns more intimately, we can be jolted into awakening. Moreover, when we can see our habits with clarity, we are enabled to question their value and can resolve to retain them, discard them, adjust them, or develop new ones, as we deem appropriate.

Once engaged compassion becomes integrated into your routine, it will feel as instinctive and comfortable as any other part of your nature. In fact, it *is* your nature. Utilizing techniques to engage compassion is not about changing the essence of who you are. Rather, it is like peeling an onion, finding your soft and gentle heart at the center, and realizing it has been there all along.

> We always have significant command over the most critical and influential elements of our lives—our minds, our manners of being, and our behaviors.

There are twenty gateways to engaged compassion, each opening a different door to greater depths of understanding. Although all can be set in motion concurrently, it is perhaps easier and far less overwhelming initially to undertake them one at a time. To some extent the gateways build upon each other. Therefore you may find it makes more sense to approach and practice them in the sequence provided. Nonetheless, feel free to adapt the order to whatever seems most suitable given your present circumstances.

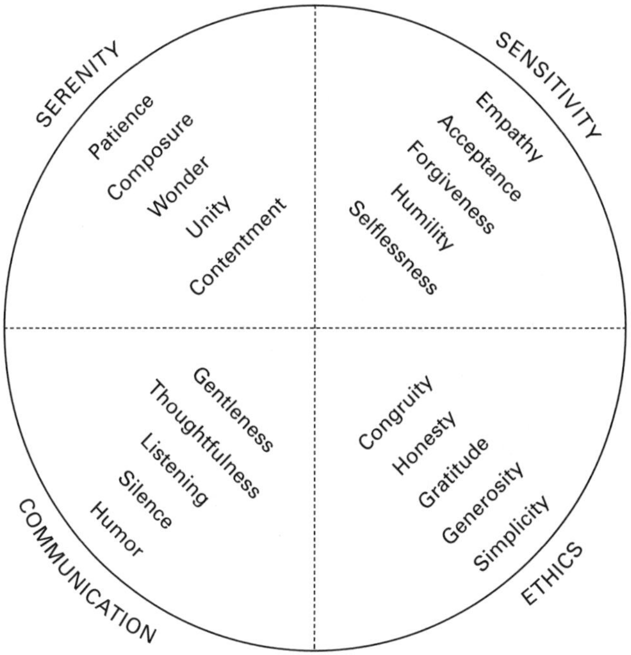

FIGURE 6.1   THE FOUR PORTALS AND TWENTY GATEWAYS

Incorporate the gateways to compassion into your life and become attentive to them. Your negative patterns will fizzle away of their own accord when more positive and productive ones replace them.

The study and implementation of engaged compassion is a lifetime endeavor. Because we are constantly changing, along with everyone and everything around us, the expression of our compassion will, by necessity, adapt. With our conscious awareness, the scope of the gateways will grow accordingly, and each time we revisit them they will seem fresh and newly energized.

THE FOUR PORTALS

The twenty gateways can be divided into four categories, or portals:

1. The portal of sensitivity
2. The portal of ethics
3. The portal of communication
4. The portal of serenity

Combined, these four portals form the foundation of a fully compassionate existence, inside and out. With the first portal, we examine the areas of our inner perspectives that can diminish or enhance our compassionate nature. With the second portal, we explore the ethical principles that guide compassionate thought and action. With the third portal, we investigate the tangible forms of compassionate expression. And with the fourth portal, we study the stream of consciousness that is extended and returned in the course of practicing engaged compassion. We will look at each of these portals and the gateways they comprise in detail in the next four chapters.

JUST BEGIN

There is no "best time" to start on the path of engaged compassion, no one moment that is better than another. Simply decide to begin, and you have begun. The compassionate way of life is available to everyone equally, regardless of age, income, education, social status, intellect, or other trifling concerns. It merely requires a hunger for truth and tranquility and a willingness to open your heart and mind.

We are all born with the fundamental skills to fully engage our compassionate nature. The gateways are only tools to help us expose and channel it constructively. Don't be concerned whether you are engaging your compassion "correctly" because there is no single "right way" to be compassionate. Your path is unique to you. It is irrelevant whether anyone else approves of it or walks before, beside, or in your footsteps.

Everything we need to know already abides within each of us. All that is left to do is get started. Just look, listen, and observe, and you will be on your way.

CULTIVATING HABIT

To fully realize your compassionate nature, engaged compassion must become a priority in your life. It needs to develop into as much of a habit as brushing your teeth or dressing appropriately for the weather. Any action can become routine when it is practiced with regularity; the same is true of compassion.

The more we exercise loving-kindness in what we think, say, and do, the stronger we will grow in our compassion. There is no other way to heal ourselves, bring peace into our hearts, and create harmony in the world. The transformation begins with each of us and is launched the moment we resolve to be seekers of awareness and truth. When we live our compassion to its fullest, we will activate it spontaneously in others. It is this simple and this complex.

79

7

The Portal
of Sensitivity

As we enter the portal of sensitivity, we are asked to leave behind our preconceptions and be willing to observe, stay open, and learn. Here we are urged to examine our hearts, emotions, and feelings and prepare for expanding our compassion beyond its ordinary bounds.

Some people equate sensitivity with feminine attributes. But both men and women, young and old, have the capacity to be receptive and tender. After all, sensitivity is merely the fusion of awareness with caring. Because we will always be at the center of our benevolence, getting to know ourselves better—from the inside out—will help us live our compassion more fully. Awakening your sensitivity and all that it encompasses is the first step in that direction.

EMPATHY

Empathy is best described as putting ourselves in another's skin. Because we can never know firsthand what others' experiences are or understand the inner workings of their emotional lives, we must use our skills of observation and imagination, along with a healthy dose of trust. To perceive suffering, deliberately focus your attention and consciously register what you see. Often someone's suffering is not immediately apparent, and the way that suffering is exhibited varies from person to person, culture to culture, and species to species. In some cultures, stoicism is the norm, so looking for overt signals of suffering may be futile. Thus it is a good idea to study subtle expressions and gestures and listen closely to what is being communicated through voice, stance, and behavior.

When you see someone in distress, imagine how you would feel if you were in a similar situation. Try to visualize yourself literally in that individual's body and circumstances. How does it feel to wear another's pain and hardships? So often we dismiss the despair of others because we think that we would never allow ourselves to get in such a predicament, or that there is a simple solution that this person has neglected to see or consider. People of privilege often view those less fortunate as not deserving of better or as having brought suffering upon themselves. Consequently, they may brush off people in need as being too ignorant, backward, or stupid to undo their plights, handily discounting or dismissing their torment.

We tend to forget that virtually all cruelties in the world, except natural disasters, are instigated by human beings, and that human kindness is the only way to reverse them. It is pointless to place blame on the sufferer or point fingers at each other. Guilt and blame are utterly useless when it comes to alleviating suffering or finding practical solutions to problems.

When we employ empathy, we can use our own knowledge of pain to relate to what someone else is going through. It isn't necessary to have experienced a comparable ordeal or identical sensations. Pain is pain, no matter if it is physical, emotional, or spiritual. Because we have all suffered in various ways, we can draw from our experiences to understand and empathize with others.

Empathy is indispensable to engaged compassion because it is the impetus for all acts of loving-kindness. Without accepting and appreciating the pain of others, there is no motivation for us to intercede. Even once we perceive another's anguish, it is tempting to turn away. Empathic people have tender spots that can be frightening and overwhelming to acknowledge. But to become wholly compassionate, we must force ourselves to look directly into the face of suffering. Only then will we see our reflections and know that the hurts of others are equal to our own.

Empathy compels us to trust that the afflictions of others are no different from ours. Even if our eyes, ears, and hearts relay conflicting messages, we still must assume that if there are *any* indications of hurt, no matter how minute, it exists and is real to those who feel it. We must also trust that all sentient beings feel pain. Because we may never be able to totally confirm the physical or emotional experiences of those with whom we cannot communicate—for instance, human infants, people with dementia, or members of other species—we ought to always err on the side of compassion. To do otherwise would be unconscionable.

When we become adept at envisioning ourselves in another's situation, we will know we are on the path to empathy. If we are unable to do this, we need to take a look at why it is difficult. Occasionally, other people's suffering strikes close to home, and allowing ourselves to feel their pain brings back a flood of raw, disturbing memories. It may be that we were never given sufficient empathy to overcome our own wounds and, in response, we have become bitter or hardened to similar suffering in others. Before we can extend empathy outward, we must validate and address our own hurts.

Acknowledge what caused your pain and take a look at the grief it has generated within you. Notice how it has settled in your body and where the aches reside. Give it your complete attention. Observe your emotions and physical reactions as you reflect on your hurt. Verbalize softly or silently to yourself what these feelings are and how they are being expressed in your body right now. Simply be aware of them. Open your heart to your sorrow and receive it lovingly, as one would embrace a child in need of reassurance and consolation. If tears well up, allow yourself to cry freely, observing their source and how it feels to release them.

We squelch our sorrows because we are afraid of them. Know that whatever sparked your pain has since passed and is powerless to harm you here in the present. Realize that your emotional scars are a precious aspect of who you are and are no less deserving of care than any other part of you. Turning your full concentration toward your hurt will, at long last, give it the attention it has craved. Once your pain has been indulged, it will no longer need to haunt you. With acceptance and confirmation, it will free you to move on in peace.

Sometimes we need help in confronting a pain-riddled past. If you find that you are unable to deal with strong emotions as they arise, you may need to seek professional assistance. It will be impossible to sincerely engage your compassion outwardly unless you fully face your own internal suffering. Enlisting the aid of a trained counselor or therapist can help you deal with your pain so that it doesn't overwhelm you or interfere with your life.

Owning up to our suffering is the greatest tool we have for engaging compassion. If we did not have our own share of sorrows, we could not empathize with the heartaches of others. We also would not have the opportunity to learn from past blunders or prevent ourselves from harming others in the same ways that we have been hurt. But our past anguish can only help us if we concede that it exists. Looking at it honestly will dissipate its control over us. Then, unfettered, we can use the insights and wisdom gained from our own travails to identify and alleviate the suffering of others.

85

ACCEPTANCE

Acceptance is born of self-respect and an appreciation for who we are despite our quirks and less-than-ideal attributes. For many people, disapproval is taught at an early age. Parents frequently push their offspring into a preconceived mold based on their own personal hopes, values, ambitions, and expectations, rather than explore what their children aspire to or where their talents and interests lie. So often young people feel pressured by family, teachers, and peers to be something other than who they are and are left feeling ashamed of and disappointed in themselves. Adding to the strain, the media and entertainment industries project flawless "role models" with impeccable bodies, exemplary personalities, and abundant time, energy, and material wealth. Surrounded by such paradigms of so-called perfection, the average individual stands little chance of developing an overly positive self-image.

Many of us have adopted knee-jerk reactions to what we consider to be our inadequacies. We mentally berate ourselves for being less than what we believe we ought to be, even though there is no conceivable way we could ever live up to the majority of our impossible longings. At the same time, we are taught that to feel good about who we are is a measure of conceit and vanity, which are equally abhorred as our imperfections. On the surface, our society advocates looking beyond superficial qualities, yet these are the very ones that are most frequently rewarded. Talk about a no-win situation!

It is difficult to feel secure in who we are when we simultaneously feel ashamed or embarrassed of ourselves. Sadly, this issue typically doesn't come to our full attention until adulthood, after we've agonized over it most of our lives. By then we have devised numerous subliminal internal messages that upbraid us each time we think we don't quite measure up to our imagined standards. Every time they play in our minds, they reinforce our negative views.

It doesn't have to be this way, however. We *can* learn to genuinely like and admire ourselves, just the way we are, without engaging in narcissism. What it takes is a fresh perspective, developing new internal responses, and practice, practice, practice.

For starters, stop comparing yourself to other people. You are unique. No one else shares your identical genetic makeup, disposition, or history. There are many ingredients and experiences that have culminated in the person you are today. Regardless of what you may do to alter your outward appearance, you will still be basically the same inside. Certainly we can—and should—take care of ourselves and our bodies by keeping fit through exercise, adequate sleep, minimizing stress, and eating healthfully. These practices will go a long way toward making us feel better about the bodies we were given. Still, if we equate self-worth with how we look on the outside, we will never be satisfied. Despite our best efforts, our bodies will eventually deteriorate and wear out, and if we entrust our happiness to our looks, joy is guaranteed to wane as well. In fact, if our pleasures in life are reliant on achieving an obscure ideal of beauty, height, weight, or other physical characteristics over which we have little control, we will be unhappy most of the time. Our bodies, like the rest of the natural world, are constantly changing—and not always in ways we would prefer—so we will never find security or continuity in them.

Just like our bodies, our personalities are in perpetual transition, too. Some days we are cheery and outgoing, while other days we are contemplative and withdrawn. Your disposition might be described as even, calm, erratic, or volatile, but in reality it is shifting all the time. We are never exclusively one temperament or another. Learning how to live with these deviations in body and mood, knowing we can never nail them down, will help us to mature in our acceptance. The more we are able to observe and endure our own fluctuations, the more we come

87

to tolerate them in others. If we aren't demanding perfection of ourselves, we are less likely to impose such an extreme criterion on others.

We all desire our work, relationships, appearance, health, and demeanors to conform to our particular visions of how they are "supposed" to be, and thoughts about them consume a considerable amount of our time. Most of us habitually obsess about them, especially in the company of others. For instance, we might wonder if we look acceptable; if our clothes are appropriate for the occasion or if they fit properly; whether what we just said makes sense or sounds sufficiently intelligent, witty, or humorous; and, of course, we usually speculate about what others are thinking about us. The irony in all this is that the people we are with undoubtedly are contemplating the very same concerns. We are *all* preoccupied with the impressions we make on those around us, regardless of who we are or the accomplishments we have achieved. Bear this in mind whenever you find yourself getting carried away with self-consciousness. You are not alone in these feelings and, quite possibly, the people you are with may be less confident than you are, despite outward appearances that seem to indicate otherwise.

People who are accepting are able to go with the flow of life. They don't resist change or become upset when their hopes are dashed because they are grounded in the moment. Acceptance understands that chasing after desires is as futile as clutching the air. It doesn't mean giving up, but it does mean giving in—surrendering to the currents of change. A rolling river gracefully swirls around a boulder in its path, continuing to move forward in spite of this obstacle. The boulder stands firm against the river's alternating tides, accommodating its unpredictable patterns. Both are able to succumb to change, to adapt and adjust without compromising their basic natures. In the midst of life's storms and surprises, we can do the same.

> Acceptance understands that chasing after desires is as futile as clutching the air.

One technique for becoming more accepting is to notice when you are evaluating yourself, to pay attention to what you are thinking so you can recognize when you are being critical. At these times, just think silently to yourself "judging . . . judging." Don't admonish yourself for being judgmental or attempt to analyze the situation. Acknowledge what you are doing, and then let it go. You may discover that you critique yourself and others a lot more frequently than you realized. When we become aware of this practice, we enable ourselves to change it. Furthermore, we can begin to see from where our negative self-esteem is emanating and how it is being continually bolstered and refueled. This can also help us identify the ways in which our positive self-esteem is persistently sabotaged.

Another method for developing greater self-acceptance is to intercept at the onset the chiding lectures and negative internal messages we repeatedly echo to ourselves. As soon as you notice one emerging, immediately start a new message that is the complete opposite of the negative one. For instance, when your mind whispers: "You bumbling fool. You always stick your foot in your mouth!" turn it around at once to be: "You are a caring person. You didn't intend to be hurtful. You did the best you were able to do at the time."

Nurture and support yourself the same way a dear friend would by providing encouragement and understanding when you let yourself or others down. There is no reason to beat yourself up over errors in judgment. This does far more harm than good. Instead, make amends to others when called for, learn by determining what you would do differently next time, and heal yourself by acknowledging that you are much more than the sum of your mistakes.

Embracing all parts of ourselves prepares us to accept the uncertainties of life and the frailties of those around us. Nevertheless, despite our best efforts, there will be times when we are intolerant or disparaging of others. We may not always be prepared for these feelings when they arise, so we need to be cognizant of how we react internally to the various people we encounter. Make a written list of the attributes that drive you crazy or taint your point of view, regardless of how petty they may seem. It is entertaining as well as instructive to see our biases in print. The only way we can become conscious of them is to dwell on them deliberately. As we admit their presence, we will become more aware of them when they occur. Again, when they arise, acknowledge them silently with the word "judging," then let them drift away and dissipate like puffs of smoke. As your prejudices are brought into clearer focus, there is little else you need to do to eradicate them. When you are ready to release them, they will dissolve like night into morning, and in their place will be a spacious well of acceptance.

To be tolerant is not the same as to be accepting. Tolerance implies endurance. We may strongly disagree with or thoroughly dislike certain people, but when we are tolerant we stomach their presence in certain situations because we think we have to or because it makes our lives easier. Acceptance means we have climbed over or out of our aversions to respect those with whom we disagree, and we are able to honor their perspectives even if we find these perspectives personally objectionable. Tolerance is offensive to people. It demeans who they are and what they believe. No one wants to be merely tolerated, but everyone wants to be accepted—not because it is the proper thing to do, but because our viewpoints and values are very important to us.

91

> Tolerance is withstanding people on *our* terms. Acceptance is embracing people on *their* terms.

Being *different* should never be equated with being *inferior*. Simply because we are unlike others, or they are unlike us, does not make either substandard. No one is "less than" anyone else. Self-appointed critics do little to ennoble themselves or enamor others, but they are quite adept at drawing attention to their own character flaws and weaknesses in the process of pointing out everyone else's.

When others sincerely respect our perspectives, we feel appreciated as human beings, regardless of whether they agree with us. We feel whole inside instead of ripped apart. We feel validated instead of defensive. In an atmosphere of mutual respect, we are able to come together with and separate from those who differ with us while keeping our, and their, dignity intact. Tolerance is withstanding people on *our* terms. Acceptance is embracing people on *their* terms.

FORGIVENESS

We are often our own worst critics. When we botch relationships, bungle opportunities, or use poor discretion, we find it almost impossible to pardon ourselves. We tend to slip repeatedly into the habit of self-reproach that many of us learned so thoroughly in childhood. As adults, why is it still so terribly hard for us to forgive?

Forgiveness and acceptance are closely intertwined, but at no time do either imply approval of cruel or unjust actions. We can and should acknowledge our wrongdoings and always try to make amends. Yet even when we let ourselves down and are disappointed in our behaviors or responses, we can continue to cherish ourselves. We all sometimes make decisions we regret. These moments of defeat, however, do not discredit our fundamental humanity. We do not automatically become "bad people" because of occasional, inadvertent breaches of conduct.

Introspection and inquiry can reveal ways to redress our infractions in nearly all circumstances. Taking every measure we can to rectify any damage or hurt we caused is the very least we can do. Sincere and timely apologies, of course, are always fitting, but usually much deeper and more tangible indications of our contrition are what is needed.

It might seem, and may very well be true, that other people pardon us more readily than we can forgive ourselves. We may also find that if we are quick to latch onto self-condemnation, we are more likely to shoulder animosity toward others whom we feel have wronged us. Forgiving ourselves is the crux of mercy and compassion. It also is essential for our own peace of mind and sanity. Harboring anger and grief can do serious emotional damage and can jeopardize our physical health as well. At the same time, it does nothing to ameliorate a rotten situation and often makes matters worse.

All human beings make mistakes. Those who are mature are able to acknowledge them and be remorseful. A true sage can learn from them and move on. Some of us, however, need to repeat our mistakes over and over until we finally fathom that the outcome isn't going to change. We all have different ways of learning. Some of us may be slower or take more circuitous routes, but we each have the potential to arrive at the same destination.

There is a bizarre feeling of self-righteousness associated with self-reproach, as if emotionally whipping ourselves will somehow erase our transgressions and elevate our sense of propriety. This belief is dangerous. Self-flagellation only makes us feel small and worthless and erodes our personal esteem. Because shame is private and inward, it has no functional capability beyond self-destruction. Although we may be reluctant to exonerate ourselves and, since we're out of practice, doing so may feel awkward, unfamiliar, and at times even inappropriate, we will not progress in our compassion or internal serenity until we do.

When you need forgiveness, turn your attention to your inner wisdom and ask for solace. To begin, simply talk to yourself silently and console your pain with heartfelt words of comfort. Speak as though you were addressing a devoted friend in

93

need. As you do, you will hear the communication of your sage within. Allow yourself the freedom to cry and express your sorrow, knowing that this part of you understands and loves you no less when you falter than when you succeed. This voice of perpetual wisdom and compassion abides with you always. As you let it speak, and as you listen, you will discover what it feels like to be forgiven and what it means to forgive.

Once we are able to vindicate ourselves and view our mistakes with greater objectivity, we will realize how to extend this grace to others. People's responses to situations are based on a complex blend of their histories, experiences, and relationships, and we can only guess at the dynamic interplay that inspires their choices. None of us can ever fully comprehend what it is like to stand in someone else's shoes. Even though we may think we know what is best for another to do, the truth is that we do not. Let's face it, if we were that amazingly astute, we wouldn't make any mistakes in our own lives! When we establish expectations to which others must aspire, we set ourselves and them up for certain disappointment.

Of course, there are times when people make egregious errors in judgment, which can have painful and irreparable consequences. When this happens, we can opt to build walls of malice and exclusion, but how would this resolve the situation? Erecting invisible bulwarks only serves to keep us isolated from others, doing much more harm to those within the fortresses than the individuals they are designed to keep out.

Animosity eats away at us from the inside out. It makes us bitter, hostile, and hard. Chances are the people with whom you are angry feel your emotional daggers only when they are in your presence. Most likely they aren't affected by your hurt when you are not around. These daggers are like boomerangs—they always return to the sender. Furthermore, what may seem like a monumental affront to you may be nothing more than a feather on their back to them.

But what if the people who have hurt you are contrite? Or what if they already feel the weight of guilt on their conscience? How will adding to their burdens improve the situation or set things right again for you, for them, or anyone else who was injured?

We are all familiar with the saying "Revenge is sweet." In reality, revenge may yield a moment of pleasure, but there is a heavy price to pay for it. When we harm another in retribution for our own pain, we cannot escape our own culpability. Anyone who knows right from wrong will be plagued with regret; it is unavoidable. When we are hurt, there is no way to equal the score without forfeiting our integrity and self-respect in the process.

We each are responsible for the suffering we cause, regardless of our motivations or any presumed justifications. Our inability to accept the volatility of life, admit our own shortcomings, and forgive the failings of others has resulted in the litigiousness of present-day society. As we seek to place blame on others and penalize them for their wrongdoings, we bury the substance of our humanity—our hearts. With insight and objectivity, we can take pity on the people who cause us suffering instead of trying to retaliate against them. People who feel a need to lash out at others do so because they feel inadequate and because they do not know any other way to relieve their frustrations. Through our examples of compassion in action, we have

95

a chance to be models of a kinder and gentler way of dealing with problems, inequity, and pain.

The golden rule of "do unto others as you would have them do unto you" is greatly adored as a slogan, but how many of us actually heed its message? This timeless expression embodies the essence of loving-kindness, and within it lie the fertile seeds of forgiveness. When we are able to release our grip on spite and indignation and reconcile even the most heinous offenses, we will comprehend what it means to wholly engage our compassion.

HUMILITY

Humility is the gentle sublimation of ego and pride. Contrary to the word's popular interpretation, it has nothing to do with false modesty. Humility is the conscious realization that we are one among many in the scheme of life. It is gaining a sense of proportion and knowing that each of us has a place and purpose. Arrogance, its inverse, extinguishes humility. The erroneous belief that we are somehow superior to others—whether people, animals, or nature herself—is what has led humanity down a slippery slope of dominance, brutality, enslavement, and destruction. When we ignore our humility, we learn how to justify practically any cruel behavior to satisfy our desires as individuals, groups, or even as an entire species.

Humility keeps us grounded. It deters us from living with a bloated ego or with our head in the clouds. When we are humble, we walk with our feet firmly planted, knowing that our imprints will inevitably fade and be lost with the passage of time.

An overfed ego swells with self-importance, and this restricts our ability to learn, grow, and be responsive. When we are so filled with ourselves, there is simply no room left to care about anyone else. Without humility, we are numbed to the pain of others. We actually come to believe in our own superiority and the rantings of an ego that tells us those who suffer are beneath us and merit nothing more than what they have.

We do not need to sacrifice personal fulfillment to invite humility into our lives. Being comfortable with who we are and satisfied with our successes is integral to a sense of self-worth. Still, we must remind ourselves that a victory in one area of life does not indicate a mastery over all the other elements of living. Rarely are our accomplishments or talents so evenly distributed. There will always be others who surpass us on certain levels and with whom we could never compete.

97

Aptitude and triumphs do not make any of us more worthy or more human. Celebrities may have more visibility, exposure, and money than most of us, but they are certainly no better, no more important, and no more valuable than anybody else. Gloating is a chance to momentarily strut our stuff, but fame, prosperity, and good fortune are fleeting. When they are gone, what will be left in their stead?

Fostering humility ensures that we will respect the abilities and achievements of others and that we will allow them to save face in moments of defeat or enjoy the spotlight even if we think we (or others) are more deserving. Humble people do not need to step on or over anyone to feel productive because they measure their wealth by how much they give rather than how much they accumulate.

Teach yourself to be humble by seeking the best in everyone. Make it a point to look for at least one admirable quality in everyone you encounter, whether it's a skill or their knowledge, style, approach to life, or wisdom. If you make even a small effort, you will find something wonderful in everybody. Focus on these qualities whenever you see or interact with people, especially those you don't really like or don't find particularly appealing. It's amazing what jewels we all possess when the digger knows how to excavate.

Humility frequently is seen as a relative quality; that is, we feel humbled only when someone else exceeds us. Most of us view humility as being put in our place, and we respond to it by trying to eclipse others or minimize their capabilities and admirable feats in an attempt to resurrect our dignity and magnify our stature. Our aversion to being less than someone else also has coerced us into amassing unlimited material wealth in a ceaseless struggle to keep up with the Joneses.

You do not need to differentiate yourself from anyone in order to be humbled, nor do you need to compete with yourself. How you fared yesterday or weeks or months ago is irrelevant to the moment at hand. Weighing your competencies, or lack of them, against your own or anyone else's will merely stoke your vanity or consume you with insecurities.

It's amazing what jewels we all possess
when the digger knows how to excavate.

When we practice staying present in the here and now, we are forced to concede the impermanence of life and all that we pride ourselves on. What we wallow in today will be gone or transformed tomorrow—possibly sooner. Even who we once thought we were has changed over time so drastically and surreptitiously that upon reflection we may not recognize our former or present selves.

Attempting to promote humility through contrasting ourselves is like trying to grab the curl of a wave. Ultimately it is senseless and counterproductive. All the same, knowing that we are fragile and small compared with the world and its transience can easily prompt us to be humble. We are each just a drop in the ocean of life. Yet, to an ocean, every drop is precious.

99

SELFLESSNESS

At first glance, it is easy to interpret selflessness as not caring about ourselves or caring about others more than ourselves. This is because when most people hear "selfless" they think "self-sacrifice." But in the context of engaged compassion, selflessness has little to do with deprivation or renunciation. Instead, it deals with our *attitudes,* rather than where or toward whom we direct our attentions, what we do, or what we possess.

Social and political activists tend to think of selflessness in terms of abdicating one's private life and personal pleasures for "the cause." Sacrifices such as these have left innumerable dedicated people miserable, burned out, and, not surprisingly, eager to resign their commitments completely.

> If we forfeit our physical, emotional, intellec-
> tual, or spiritual health for the sake of others,
> we diminish the value of all life in general,
> because we have diminished our own.

We cannot sever a vital branch of compassion without imbalancing what remains of ourselves, and practicing engaged compassion necessitates that we remain whole. If the core of engaged compassion is cherishing who we are, to forego this would be a total dissolution of our empathic nature. Compassion not only depends on us meeting our own needs, it insists upon it. This cannot be emphasized strongly enough. If we forfeit our physical, emotional, intellectual, or spiritual health for the sake of others, we diminish the value of all life in general because we have diminished our own. To be fully compassionate, we must honor and respect ourselves and our needs no less than those of any other life.

Selflessness pertains to how we regard others as we go about our daily tasks or reach out expressly in the spirit of engaged compassion. It is a matter of perspective, intention, and approach. In terms of benefiting or doing damage to ourselves and others, it is perhaps far better to do nothing than to do something reluctantly or with a negative attitude. Selflessness also is concerned with the *impetus* behind our actions. If we engage in activities to inflate our egos, feel good about ourselves, or impress somebody, our motivations are selfish, not selfless. With selflessness, we immerse ourselves in tasks solely to do what we believe is right and kind. When entered into egolessly, selfless work bestows contentment through the knowledge that we are giving wholeheartedly to aid another.

It is important to remember that selflessness is smothered by a patronizing posture. To give in earnest, we must regard those in need as our equals and offer the same respect to them that we hope others would give to us. We are all just a heartbeat away from asking for help. The grace we extend today may be just what we are in need of tomorrow. Sincere benevolence compels us to ensure that the dignity of those we assist remains intact.

Some people are concerned that selflessness must entail renouncing one's identity or losing oneself to a crusade, as one might to a monastic religious order. In practice, we find that just the opposite is true. Selfless actions beget a sense of empowerment, freedom, and confidence that fosters a better understanding of who we are and where and how we fit in.

When we participate in selfless acts we are liberated from the boundaries of fear and manipulation that our egos use to alienate us from others. Through this emancipation, we can transcend ordinary time and space and more fully experience life. We can connect with and relate to others more completely, because we are not concerned about their judgments of us. Selflessness obliges us to abandon our insecurities and frees us from the constraints of diffidence and self-consciousness.

101

Selflessness presents a golden opportunity to discover who we are while we deliberately suspend the search.

Selfless acts draw people together. There is an unspoken camaraderie that develops among those who participate in gifts of selflessness. Imagine a group of strangers coming together to paint someone's house, pick up litter from a park, feed stray cats, stuff envelopes for a mailing, or prepare a shared meal, and you can see how individual differences are dissolved by the common thread of dynamic caring.

At no time do we have a greater chance of feeling purposeful than when we are helping others in the spirit of compassion. It is a golden opportunity to discover who we are while we deliberately suspend the search. When we cease looking for our true selves and yield to the spirit of giving, our true selves will find us. You can recognize yours by the joy reflected in the eyes of those around you and by the deep, warming sense of satisfaction that you feel after giving your all and doing your best in the course of altruistic service. Even at our lowest points we can feel a surge of energy and renewed hope by performing deeds of loving-kindness. Selfless generosity is one of the few feats that can pull us up from self-pity or out of the depths of depression. It can give us a glimmer of nirvana, the peacefulness that comes from within when motivation, attitude, and action are, for one magical moment, aligned.

8

The Portal
of Ethics

Virtually all the people I have ever known consider themselves to be ethical. I would speculate that even the most
hardened criminals believe they have strong principles, and I'd
wager that, at least on certain levels, they do. Humanity's problems, personally and globally, don't stem from a shortage of
ethics. Rather, they are the result of ethics being repressed, distorted, or selectively applied.

Ethics are the moral standards we uphold when nobody
else is watching. The portal of ethics invites us to explore this
realm so we can gain more insight into our convictions and
understand how to employ them evenly and constructively, both
publicly and privately.

CONGRUITY

Every day, nearly every moment, we encounter thoughts, situations, and relationships that challenge our ethics. Our minds are always churning, so most of us are continually weighing our choices and making decisions that include at least an element of principled evaluation. Thus it may be maddening to hear that we may not be quite as ethical as we'd like to believe we are.

> Ethics are the moral standards we uphold when nobody else is watching.

To one extent or another we all make exceptions for our ethics. We may bend the rules a little or disregard what we usually would value in order to reduce the pressure of an uncomfortable predicament or obtain something we strongly desire. I'd venture to say that few of us feel we are betraying our ethics when we do this, but each time we tweak our values to accommodate our circumstances, rather than the other way around, we lose a bit of our integrity in the process. There seems to be an endless supply of "just this once" occasions, so much so that we rarely, if ever, pay attention to them and may not even be aware that we are compromising ourselves and our values.

The most egregious self-deceptions occur when we engage in behaviors that are completely contrary to what we espouse, yet, on some level, we allow ourselves to believe they are totally acceptable. An example of this is when we rationalize cruelty or combat in the name of religion, politics, democracy, economics, justice, or peace. Sometimes we don't even question what we are doing because we have already intellectually reconciled it with our consciences. At other times we may pass off issues as somebody else's problem, especially if they don't fit neatly into our ideas of what is meaningful or important. Or we might presume "There's nothing I can do about this anyway," or "My efforts won't make a dent," so we call it quits before we even try to make a difference.

This is what makes living a wholly compassionate life so interesting and vitally rewarding. When we commit to fully engaging our compassion, we pledge to thoroughly scrutinize everything we think, say, and do. As we proceed, we will inevitably uncover rough terrain and washed-out bridges along with fertile fields and sunny skies. It is not a painless undertaking because we all have inconsistencies in our lives, buried bigotries, and tainted perceptions.

There will be times when you are tempted to quickly push aside alternative points of view or refuse to analyze parts of your life that you are reluctant to change. Even so, try not to be so hasty. There probably are many beliefs you hold as truth today that previously seemed preposterous to you. To move forward, allow yourself to remain open, spacious, and receptive to alternative beliefs because you may very well choose to adopt them as your own—if not now, perhaps sometime down the road. There is no logical reason to shut out or automatically discredit new ideas and possibilities. They aren't a threat. You always have the choice to consider them, accept them, toss them aside, or keep them on hold to revisit another day.

When we compartmentalize our ethics and appoint them to particular parts of our lives but not to others, we miss manifold opportunities to activate compassion. Even if we think that

105

certain aspects of daily living are irrelevant to compassion, there is probably a much greater link than we initially are able or willing to see.

Most of us would agree that we care about fair trade and labor practices, racial and gender equality, safeguarding the environment, protecting animals and other wildlife, and conserving rainforests and wetlands. But few of us genuinely consider these matters when making everyday decisions and purchases. We want our choices to be a good example to others, but where do we draw the line? Comfort? Convenience? Conformity? Price? Fashion? Status? Are your inclinations based on compassion, or do you invest more heavily in self-gratification and what others might think of you?

Our personal and business relationships, occupations, clothing, cosmetics, body care products, household cleaners, food selections, modes of transportation, housing, furniture, investments, politics, hobbies, charitable work, recreational activities, and more can be significant expressions of our compassion, if we choose to inspect them closely. Tragically, few people are willing to question the ethics of these myriad aspects of life that we generally take for granted. Our culture trains us not to rock the boat, and our families, friends, and colleagues usually echo this sentiment.

It's true that taking a keen look at our ordinary alliances and activities can be intimidating because there is no doubt we will find elements both large and small that need improvement. We make endless excuses for not wanting to change. Topping the list is usually "It's too much effort," although there are many other common apologies as well. Is complacency really a defensible argument for not furthering our compassion? Do we truly have the right to call ourselves compassionate if we deliberately turn our backs on making wiser and kinder choices?

There are many ways we are erratic in our compassion, but we will not be able to become consistent until we commit to taking a critical look at our lifestyles—not just one or two isolated segments but everything. Evaluate how you treat friends, family, coworkers, children, companion animals, and strangers. Think before you purchase items and determine where and how they were made, whether you truly need them, and how they will affect others and the environment in the short and long runs. Explore whether animals and people suffered or died for your food, entertainment, cosmetics, cleaners, clothing, jewelry, or shoes. Do your pastime activities seem benign on the surface but contain hidden suffering when you delve more deeply? Do you inadvertently support war, hate, oppressive labor practices, or environmental degradation through your financial ventures, memberships, or other affiliations?

> All aspects of our lives are interconnected, entwined with each other and with all living beings and the earth.

As practitioners of engaged compassion, we must examine all the cracks and crevices of our lives and make every attempt to become aware of areas we neglect. There is hypocrisy in standing up for specific points of compassion while willfully disregarding others. All aspects of our lives are interconnected, entwined with each other and with all living beings and the

107

earth. There are many seemingly small but tremendously significant repercussions that occur when we refuse to probe exten-
sively into our hearts and actions.

Modern living is complex and fast paced, and as individuals we may never achieve our compassionate ideals. Nevertheless, if we slow down long enough to truly live and feel each
moment, with diligence and awareness we can move ever closer
to congruity.

HONESTY

Honesty is held in high esteem in our culture, yet nearly everyone, it seems—from the highest public officials to clergy, from
friends to our family and ourselves—has at times told white lies
or been otherwise less than forthright. Some of us interpret
honesty to mean that we must spill our guts and tell everything
to everyone regardless of the consequences. Others believe we
have the right, even the obligation, to give friends and family
our honest opinions, whether or not they are solicited. Still others think that what is considered honest is always changing,
evolving, depending on the circumstances, and that honesty is
really a continuum of truthfulness.

Truth is what we see when we look without judgment.
Usually when we say we are being honest, we are actually just
being opinionated. The truths we offer are, in reality, our beliefs
and values. With this in mind, can what we call truth ever be
unequivocal? If not, then is it possible for any of us to legiti-
mately fathom truth?

Truth is what we see when we look without judgment.

Most of the time we are not truthful, especially with ourselves. This is not necessarily deliberate. We often are not truthful because we frequently aren't clear about or in touch with what we are feeling, particularly if we are flustered, mired in intense emotion, pressured, or in the middle of a perturbing situation. If we can't be honest with ourselves, we can't expect to be honest with others. When we are perplexed by our emotions, we cannot be certain that our choices are the best ones for us or anyone else who might be affected by them, and we can't be positive that what we tell others is indeed "the truth." Stressful, heated, or confusing interactions necessitate a cooling-off period, time to detach from the tension to gain perspective and neutrality.

The accompanying picture contains two images. Can you see them both?

109

Figure 8.1

Depending on how you focus, you see a pedestal (or vase, candlestick, or goblet) or the silhouette of two faces. Because of how our minds operate, we are capable of seeing only one of the two images in the picture at a time, even though they both exist simultaneously. Some people look at this rendering and are able to detect only one of the images but not the other, and there are people who cannot discern either one. Who is right? It depends, of course, on who is doing the looking and that person's mindset at the time.

Everything we see, feel, and do is filtered through our worldviews. Nothing is perceived quite the same by another individual. Rarely is there one side, or even two, to any given event. There are multiple sides and infinite ways of construing what we experience. Nothing in our lives is solidly true. Everything tangible is continually changing, so our perceptions are constantly shifting, too. Truth is only "truth" as we know it from our own judgmental standpoint as it exists at this moment. In the next moment it might very well be altered. As we evolve, so will our understanding of any particular "truth."

Because we cannot be honest with other people if we are incapable of being honest with ourselves, the quest for candor must begin in a private, inward way. Every moment is pregnant with opportunity to find the kernel of truth it conceals. We can use our powers of awareness, observation, objectivity, and sensitivity to begin to uncover truth and see it more clearly. When we do, we will recognize it not by intellectualization or the power of reasoning, but through the modest articulation of our hearts.

Honesty is truth tempered with tact and compassion. It requires the ability to identify the *universal truths* that are obscured

by ego, passion, and materialism. Universal truths are discon-
nected from our earthly perspectives. They have nothing to do
with assumption, dogma, or personal sentiment. One way to distinguish universal truth from secularistic opinion is that truth
does not hurt; it simply abides. Honesty, in the context of engaged
compassion, engenders neither malice nor the intent to degrade,
punish, embarrass, shame, or manipulate. Truth exists for its own
purposes, and each of us is capable of discovering it.

If you feel compelled to speak your mind and your dis-
closure injures someone else, you are not being honest within
the framework of compassion; you are only taking advantage of
furthering your own agenda. There is never a defensible occasion that we owe it to ourselves or to others to express painful
viewpoints under the pretext of being honest. By doing so, we
steal their dignity by presuming they weren't astute enough to
perceive as well as we can. Hurtful revelations shielded by a veil
of "truthfulness" are cowardly. They imply that the individual we
are addressing knows far less than we do or has perceptions that
are twisted or retarded.

111

> One way to distinguish universal truth from
> secularistic opinion is that truth does not
> hurt; it simply abides.

In the realm of engaged compassion, honesty is liberating.
It feels satisfying and is enlightening. It does not have hidden
motives, and its appearance is joyful and soothing, not disturbing.

When people say they are just being honest, but their comments sting or cause anguish, remember that this is not honesty, it is arrogance. At the same time, when you feel the urge to tell it like it is, think about what you will say beforehand. Consider the consequences of such "truth" and reflect on the meanings of compassion and honesty in advance. Once words leave our lips or are sent in correspondence, they cannot be retrieved; we will never be able to unring the bell and take them back.

Honesty is the unpretentious manifestation of universal truths. Anything short of this is deception. Anything exceeding it is beyond words.

GRATITUDE

In our culture of extreme plenty, even those of us who have abundance clamor for more than we need. We tend to focus on what we wish we had rather than the bounty that is right in front of us. We are inclined to feel inferior if it appears that everyone around us is collecting the latest gadgets, gizmos, or status possessions that we do not have. We are fearful that our children will fall behind or become out of step with their peers if we don't succumb to the pressures by free enterprise to overindulge them. Many of us even depend on these external acquisitions to buoy our self-esteem and make us feel important or successful in life.

Imagine for a minute that you've lost all that you own— your home, car, clothing, jewelry, electronic devices, books, photographs, musical recordings, instruments, artwork, and sentimental objects. What is left in your life that truly holds value for you? Most people say, "My health is the most important consideration," or "As long as my loved ones are safe and alive, the rest doesn't matter." But on a day-to-day basis, it *does* matter. Our loved ones simply are not enough to fulfill our cravings, which is one reason we keep resorting to accumulating more stuff. We often are so busy earning money to buy more stuff that we struggle to maintain our mental and physical health, and the very loved ones we say we treasure are regularly slighted.

In the bustle of daily living, we generally fantasize about what we wish we had that would make our lives feel more complete. We daydream about a bigger house, a newer or larger car, a different body shape, more fashionable clothing, elegant jewelry, improved fitness or health, the latest computer, more free time, a lover or life mate, or something else that we think would make us feel more whole or make our lives more perfect. While we are imagining what it would be like if our hopes were actualized, we lose touch with the present moment and become disengaged with what are, in reality, our fundamental priorities.

Imagine for a minute that you've lost all that you own. What is left in your life that truly holds value for you?

What is genuinely meaningful to us we already have: our precious lives and the abilities to breathe, see, hear, move, touch, respond, feel, cry, think, communicate, smile, and laugh. These gifts hold a lifetime of exploration, experimentation, and exhilaration.

When we realize this and actually grasp it on a visceral level, we know that there is very little else we need to fulfill us or adorn our lives. But how often do we pay attention to these riches, dwell on them, use them wisely or to their fullest, and are grateful for them?

For the most part, we take them for granted and don't consciously think about them. Because we have always had them, we just figure we always will. When we study these gifts and become aware of how integral they are to our happiness, and how limited and empty we would be without them, we can see that all else pales in comparison.

Conscious awareness facilitates the recognition of our vital abilities. When you intentionally note what your body is doing—which parts are moving and how—or what you are thinking, seeing, or touching, you can begin to make your waking hours a meditation in thankfulness. Noticing how you are breathing, what sensations you feel physically, or which emotions you are experiencing will assist you in staying present and being appreciative.

Gratitude and humility go hand in hand. When we are humble, we can concede that we do not inherently deserve more than any other sentient being. Therefore, we can be grateful that we have all that we need to sustain us. Humility helps us to cherish what we have and be satisfied with it, to admit that what we have is enough. It is a reminder of our relationship with the rest of humanity and the larger community of life. Although our intangible gifts are ephemeral—which makes them all the more precious—they serve us more faithfully and fruitfully than the tangible belongings we dream about. If we did not have our senses and abilities to think, feel, and enjoy, material acquisitions would be utterly useless.

Our lives are rich with endless beauty and cheer, but when we are scrambling to maintain an impossible pace, we don't take the time to notice. Every day the venerable sun warms and enlivens us, the sky blushes shades of blue and gray, clouds shift in density and shape, trees and flowers sheath the earth in continual stages of birth and death, hillsides loom, birds soar and serenade, air currents waft soft aromas, winds billow and fade, the moon stalks the sun, and the stars peek from behind the black-blue canopy that materializes with a hush each night. We know that the natural world exists around us and that we experience an irrepressible joy when we comprehend that we are a part of it. Still, how often do we watch it, become involved with it, or even acknowledge its presence? Can we find what there is to be grateful for in the midst of an overcast day, the pall of winter, or the gloom of night as readily as we can in the bloom of spring or luminescence of summer?

115

When we are thankful, we are filled with appreciation, and there is no room left for envy and wishful thinking. Instead, we are bathed in the bliss of contentment. If we put our minds to the task, we can find something to be grateful for even in the most dire situations or heartrending circumstances. Our problems and challenges are opportunities for learning in disguise, and so even in the midst of difficulties we can be thankful for the chance to grow and stretch our heart muscles.

> When we are thankful, we are filled with appreciation, and there is no room left for envy and wishful thinking.

Each morning when you arise, think of something or someone that graces your life with gladness. It could be the gift of a good night's sleep, the kindness of your partner, the sunrise, your morning meal, a comfortable home, a satisfying job, your health, your companion animals, a special skill or talent, the trees, a dear friend, or your very life itself. Each night when you retire, think of yet another gift in your life. Breathe in the peace and happiness that these gifts impart, and breathe out your gratitude and appreciation to them and all the world. Let the joy of your blessings fill your heart and every cell of your body with thankfulness and serenity. Then, with a calm and grateful heart, embrace the emerging day or drift into peaceful slumber with a smile.

Our inward expressions of gratitude are an indispensable aspect of our happiness and are integral to our general sense of contentedness. The outward articulation of gratitude, however, is an absolutely essential part of every mutually rewarding relationship with other people. Too often we think that the goodness we receive is simply what is "expected" or "deserved," so no pronouncement of thankfulness is necessary. How untrue! The most valued contribution we can make to the happiness of others—children or adults, regardless of stature—is to demonstrate our heartfelt appreciation of them. It doesn't matter if we thank them for a cherished keepsake, a thoughtful gesture, or just for being the wondrous people that they are. Appreciation is the one gift that everyone longs for and treasures unequivocally over all others. It is also something for which we never outgrow the need.

> No word in any language reverberates quite as sweetly as the sound of our own name.

When you express gratitude to others, call them by their name. There is no word in any language that reverberates quite as sweetly as the sound of our own name. Using people's names is a way to demonstrate the sincerity of your appreciation, to draw attention to others as individuals, and to communicate in a meaningful manner.

A show of sincere gratitude takes so little time, costs nothing, and in no way detracts from our own self-worth. In fact, our spirits are enhanced merely by enriching another's. It feels good—no, it feels great!—to make someone else feel good. In your waking hours you have endless opportunities to demonstrate your appreciation. By taking advantage of them as often as possible, you can engage your compassion effortlessly and exuberantly, while simultaneously spreading an aura of welcome and good cheer in your path.

GENEROSITY

In cultures that emphasize personal autonomy and individual entitlement over solidarity and fellowship, it is not surprising to discover that sharing is an anomaly and that there is a gross disparity in the distribution of wealth. The opposites of generosity are greed, hoarding, and gluttony, and they are staggeringly prevalent in our society.

As nations, groups, and individuals, we cling to abundance as a mode of domination. When we regulate principal resources, we have command over those who desperately need them. Although it is a false and fleeting mastery, it can temporarily provide a heady sense of power. This feeling of control can be intoxicating and addicting. It makes us feel invigorated, stimulated, and larger than life itself. It can dupe us into believing in our own personal greatness and delude us into thinking we have the ability to defeat even death.

We accrue excess material goods primarily for two reasons: to induce a feeling of self-permanence and to inspire a sense of euphoria. Power, bliss, and life are short-lived. No matter what we may do to try to change this, we will only be frustrated in our efforts. Our attempts to bypass the reality of impermanence will always fail us miserably and leave us with perpetual agitation, dread, and sadness. Authority dissipates. Elation evaporates. Life terminates. In the end, we are merely mortal, and each of us is subject to the same eventual demise. No amount of opulence can prevent the inevitable. Underneath our ostentatious accumulations, we are all shivering, naked, and vulnerable.

Collecting material goods makes us feel solid, if ever so briefly. It masks our fears of being temporal, of losing all that we think we are and own. It also seduces us into believing we are more deserving, more worthy, more loved, and more important than those who have less than we do. Regardless of how much we acquire, possessions can never fill our hearts or satisfy our longings for spiritual truth. When we attempt to suppress our apprehensions and aversions through the accumulation of personal effects, we transform our so-called belongings into false deities. Our supposed good fortunes are little more than a very private ball and chain because we are responsible for and must take care of all that we possess.

When we have just a bit, every bit matters. Even if we have very little, we can be ingenious in our benevolence. Philanthropy of the heart does not depend on material assets but rather on the nobleness of the spirit. Real generosity is when our longings to help another supersede our desires for self-indulgence.

Giving smarts, at least just a twinge, even when it is something we wholeheartedly want to do. If it doesn't make a difference to us whether we part with something, we cannot call our offering truly "generous." With gifts of compassion, the sting of sharing is profoundly offset by the solace of doing what we know in our hearts to be morally right. Giving becomes its own reward, and our personal pleasures from doing so are secondary and irrelevant.

The bite of honest giving is momentary and does not cause suffering for the giver or the receiver. The purpose of giving is to *relieve* suffering, not create more. People who suffer in the course of being generous are seeking martyrdom, not selflessness.

> Real generosity is when our longings to help another supersede our desires for self-indulgence.

Compassionate giving refers not only to the tangible but to the intangible, known as "generosity of the spirit." In this

119

sense, no matter how much or how little we materially possess, we all have an unlimited capacity to be generous.

The gifts that mean the most to others are those that are given freely from the heart with no strings attached, not even the hope of a thank you. The barometer for generosity is whether it impinges on our personal desires—be they related to time, finances, or comfort—and if we can honestly say we have no expectations. Only when these two criteria are met can we rightfully call our actions "generous." And only when our actions are sincerely generous will we experience the abstruse peace of selfless giving.

120

SIMPLICITY

Often when people hear the word "simplicity" they think it refers to being a simpleton, or being impoverished, or living an austere life devoid of joy. Yet the simple life is inherently rich in ways an affluent lifestyle never can be. Simplicity involves stripping away all that is unnecessary and living without excess, so that we are able to see, hear, and feel life unobstructed and unencumbered. It means paring down to the core, to the bare bones of your spirit.

Materialism insulates our hearts from being touched by others. It encases us in a false sense of security and prominence and blurs our vision of what is real. When we are unhappy, we can retreat to a world of money and objects to numb our pain. We can immerse ourselves in extravagance, travel, or preoccupations designed to anesthetize our woes. But these brief euphoric surges always end as abruptly as they begin. There is no resolution to the painful feelings and therefore no substantial or authentic relief. The letdown smacks us hard and leaves us feeling even more achy and empty than before. These bitter blows provoke us into immediately resuming the futile search for a permanent means to emotional paralysis through escape. Materialism is a vicious, endless cycle that inhibits us from living *in* the moment and instead encourages living *for* the moment.

Simplicity casts off the phony shields that separate us from ourselves and others. It makes the whole of life more splendid and more real. Simplicity gives us the independence to feel our emotions fully, to submerge ourselves in them and thoroughly experience them so we can release them or invite them to become a part of us. In lieu of mindless diversions or breaking away into oblivion, the simple life advocates living in the moment with nothing to distract us.

121

> Materialism is a vicious, endless cycle that inhibits us from living *in* the moment and instead encourages living *for* the moment.

With living simply, there are none of the soaring highs that materialism champions, but there are none of the devastating lows, either. Simplicity inspires us to walk the path between these two extremes and locate the middle ground, the place where happiness resides.

Whenever we acquire material things, we need the motivation and means to take care of them; otherwise they will deteriorate and become completely worthless. Maintaining our accumulations requires a lot of mental and physical energy, not to mention financial resources. If we are emotionally attached to our effects in any way, they suck away our freedom as well. Materialism constrains our lives to revolve around the upkeep of our possessions—storing, repairing, cleaning, and displaying them. Our "things" hamper our ability to be mobile, to pick up and move whenever and wherever we might like. They restrict our housing options, cut into our spare time, and even put demands on our relationships. The more we accrue, the more space our stuff takes up, physically and emotionally, and the more heavily we are weighed down.

Living simply can be exciting. In a culture mired in abundance, it is actually a pleasure to see how much we can do without. There is an exhilarating sense of liberation in extricating ourselves from needless waste. There also is a feeling of pith and dimension to a life lived with spiritual substance over corporeal trappings.

Do not make the common error of equating simplicity with being destitute. There are drastic differences between the two. People who choose to live simply make a conscious decision to do so. They are not denying themselves the essentials of life—food, clothing, and shelter. Rather, they are electing to do without superfluous luxuries that are so often mistaken for necessities. On the other hand, few people decide to be indigent. Poverty is not an enviable situation for anyone. The major distinctions between indigence and simplicity are that the former entails deprivation and the latter involves minimalism with sufficiency. In addition, there is always the matter of self-determination. People who pursue simplicity do so deliberately. Poverty, however, is never intentional nor desirable.

Although we can simplify our lives on many levels, most people begin with their physical surroundings by culling out useless belongings and refusing to purchase anything that isn't genuinely needed. Extraneous items might be given away to family, friends, shelters for the unhoused, or thrift shops. Some people hold yard sales or donate particular items to charitable organizations. When we need something, we can choose to buy it secondhand or recycled and minimize our purchases of newly made wares. We can opt to take public transportation, if that is feasible, or walk or ride a bicycle. We can cook our own food instead of regularly eating out, and we can resolve to eat more modestly. We can reduce or eliminate our television viewing, cut back or halt our magazine and catalog subscriptions, and vow not to become slaves to the latest technology. If we dig deeply enough, we can find countless facets of our lives that could be simplified without curtailing our enjoyment.

As we cut away the surplus and nonessentials, we are able to focus more intently on what remains. We are freer to ascertain what is most important to us and to what we truly would like to devote ourselves. We can see where our time and energies have been sapped and can reclaim and redirect them. The colors in our lives will seem brighter, our relationships more precious, the natural world more vibrant, and the intangible more dear.

A simple life emancipates our spirits from their earthly clutches so that they can soar unimpeded. Without being shackled by needless accoutrements, our compassion is liberated as well.

9

The Portal
of Communication

Like all people, you communicate in a wide range of ways: the timbre and inflection of your voice, the content of what you say, your gestures, posture, eye contact, actions, and even the cadence of your speech and rapidity of your movements. Your overall style of communication is a mix of your inherited traits, physical capabilities, upbringing, acquired habits, persona, and intentions. These individual idiosyncrasies are so much a part of each of us that we generally pay very little attention to them. We sincerely believe that how we communicate is simply a part of our personalities, so we rarely think about changing it. All the same, there are a number of good reasons why we should take a serious look at how we express ourselves.

Regardless of what you actually say, your tone of voice and affectations can belie the honesty of your words. Many of us often end up conveying messages we did not mean to impart. Even without speaking, we unintentionally transmit a great deal because our mannerisms and facial expressions are powerful communicators themselves.

Sometimes we feel misunderstood or are baffled by people's responses to us. It's easy to shrug it off as their faulty impressions, but it's highly likely they were reading us correctly and we were simply sending out mixed signals. To express yourself clearly and accurately, pay close attention to what you are communicating in all the various modes at your disposal. By doing so, you can save yourself and others needless upset and confusion and can be assured you are not confounding what you want to relate.

GENTLENESS

There are many people who have the most benign intentions but are unable to get this across in what they say and do. They may bark when they speak or be blunt, terse, or indifferent, and this gruff exterior negates their well-meant aims. Other people may slam doors, pound their desks, or create general commotion. How often have you seen someone enter a room with the clear objective of stealing all the attention? A booming voice or thundering presence overruns other people and stomps them into oblivion. People who are loud, caustic, icy, or overbearing often do not consciously realize they are quashing, intimidating, or alienating others. Nevertheless, their brusque behaviors, barbed words, bravado, sarcasm, sharp intonations, or frosty aloofness give the impression that within some part of their psyches they believe they are more important than those around them.

Gentleness does not equal submissiveness or spinelessness, but it does entail an awareness of and sensitivity to others. Being gentle smooths and softens our craggy edges so we don't injure ourselves or others with unkind thoughts or hurtful actions or by using our tongues as weapons. It will not, however, recast our basic character. Irrespective of your nature—outgoing, energetic, humorous, reserved—gentling yourself will only round your jagged corners, not change your fundamental personality.

When we pointedly invade others' spaces—whether physically, verbally, or psychologically—we are declaring that they are nonentities and we are omnipotent. It doesn't matter if this is not our deliberate objective or what we actually feel; it is what is communicated nonetheless. A more subdued, moderate, and inviting approach can still get our messages across while accommodating our temperaments, but it will do so without overwhelming those in our paths. Because being gentle does not necessitate compromising our elemental selves, there is absolutely no risk involved and nothing for us to lose except our thorniness.

127

> Being gentle smooths and softens our craggy edges so we don't injure ourselves or others.

Gentleness is the embodiment of our tender and respectful feelings toward people and all life. Gentleness is conceived in our hearts and is articulated through our speech, stance, and assertive and responsive behaviors. It calls for us to walk in peace through the forest of life, keeping our footsteps light, our actions unobtrusive, and our voices calm and soft.

Your manner of being mirrors who you are inside; therefore, gentleness must begin from within. Feigning tenderness on the outside will not generate an internal transformation. Such change always occurs the other way around. Thus it will be impossible to sustain an air of gentleness if it is disingenuous. Sooner or later something in your demeanor will give you away.

> Gentleness calls for us to walk in peace through the forest of life, keeping our footsteps light, our actions unobtrusive, and our voices calm and soft.

Foster gentleness by candidly appraising your behavior, the pitch of your voice, your carriage, and your mien, and consider in what ways they might be construed as intrusive, abrasive, steely, domineering, or squelching. Try to detach from your ego so you can step back and gain a clearer perspective. If you find this is too difficult to do objectively, enlist the aid of a trusted friend or two whom you feel will be forthright with you. Even with these outside opinions, you will need to decide for yourself if you can accept your friends' truths as your own. Regardless of who does the evaluating, there will always be blind spots and the continual challenge of remaining impartial. So take what you can use from these external assessments, but still conduct an inquiry of your own.

It is always fascinating and usually eye-opening to learn what others think about us and how we come across. Here are some questions to ask yourself or those you recruit to help you as you work on getting a handle on your communication style:

- Which adjectives most accurately describe my voice quality and tone?
- What words characterize my general disposition and demeanor?
- Is my persona disarming, warm, prickly, distant, or cold?
- Are people relaxed, open, confident, and trusting around me, or do they seem apprehensive, bothered, or withdrawn?
- Do people appear agitated or distressed in my presence, or do I have a soothing and calming affect on them?

Understanding how we are perceived is the first step in gentling our ways. It could be that people see us as cool and composed while inside we are constantly churning. Or it might be the inverse; we appear surly and irascible, when inside we feel sedate and collected. The purpose of analyzing the impressions we make is to reconcile our own mental images of ourselves with the ones others have of us. We can then make adjustments accordingly. In order to gentle and align our inner and outer selves, we need to overcome the discrepancies between who we *think* we are and who we *really* are.

Gentleness also encompasses how we solve problems and which methods we resort to when we are angry, defensive, or conflicted. From a behavioral standpoint, gentleness is the essence of nonviolence. When we focus on choosing the most compassionate words and gentlest solutions, we are naturally drawn toward those that will inspire peaceful communications, considerate relationships, and amicable outcomes.

Both what we say and how we say it wield much power. Sometimes words that seem innocuous to us can cause others to bristle or be repelled. Be aware of your words and how they might be construed as scurrilous or inflammatory. Avoid using terms of endearment, such as honey, baby, dear, sweetie, or sweetheart, with colleagues, subordinates, acquaintances, or strangers. Although these expressions may seem harmless, they can be demeaning, patronizing, and embarrassing and are best reserved for intimate relationships.

In the course of evaluating your outward demeanor, reflect on how you respond internally as well. How do you handle your own disappointments and blunders? What do you do to brace yourself in the face of challenge and defeat? How do you mollify fear or assuage self-directed anger? To be balanced in our tenderness, we must gentle our inward discourse at the same time we determine how to deal more kindly with others.

As we focus on outward and inward gentleness, our dispositions will grow more even and we will find ourselves less volatile, moody, and erratic. With further introspection, we can become proactive—thinking before we speak or act—instead of reactive—responding without forethought. When we regularly contemplate gentleness, we greatly enhance the likelihood of making serene choices.

A comprehensive and abiding awareness of your communication style, combined with a genuine desire to be more compassionate, are the only tools you need to activate your gentler side. As you remain cognizant of how you communicate, not just the substance of what you say and do, and the intent behind your interactions, you will be able to determine where, when, and how you need to inject more gentleness.

COURTESY AND THOUGHTFULNESS

Virtually every culture has protocols for respectful behavior. Some customs may be unlike anything we have been exposed to, but they are no less valid and valued by their communities. It may seem that decorum serves little purpose other than to stifle our personal freedom of expression. But as we probe more deeply, we can see that courtesy and etiquette have numerous objectives, not the least of which are maintaining harmony, delineating roles, and demonstrating respect.

131

Good old-fashioned manners compel us to exhibit deferential behavior toward others, independent of our personal opinions of them. For instance, in Western cultures it is customarily polite to offer your seat to an elder, to hold open the door for the person behind you, to say "please" when you make a request, to apologize when you err, or to say "thank you" when someone helps you. These are the standards of our society, so we expect that they and countless other formalities will be honored. When they are disregarded, people are taken aback and they feel personally offended and impugned.

Essential courtesies help people save face, and therefore they are instrumental in maintaining peace. Being mannerly has nothing to do with one's station in life. It is simply a matter of implementing the common conventions of respect that are accepted and employed by the culture at large. In terms of engaged compassion, it makes sense to comply with these standards of propriety. Displays of respect make people feel good, plain and simple, and spreading good cheer is one of the primary purposes of engaged compassion.

As seekers of the compassionate way, our aim is to relieve suffering, but we must be cognizant of what remains once the suffering is removed. Instead of a gaping hole, it is essential that we ensure a fulfilling sense of gladness is left behind. Using social graces as a paradigm, we can structure our conduct to demonstrate the respect that is initiated and engendered by ordinary, everyday civility.

Courtesy has its limitations, however, as it is restricted solely to prescribed conduct dictated by social customs. It does not lead us to contemplate the deeper implications of respectful behavior, nor does it inspire us to ponder motivations outside the domain of cultural conformity. For many people, courteous gestures are rote and devoid of genuine emotion. When our actions are mechanical, they are performed out of habit and are enacted with little or no premeditation. Contrarily, engaged compassion enlists courtesy as a powerful mode of expressing lovingkindness and respect. It is planned, sought after, and intentional.

Nevertheless, in spite of its importance, courtesy is not the only form that compassionate consideration takes. Once we step outside the gate of customary social norms, we discover innumerable pathways that lead to the realm of *thoughtfulness*. Here respect is elevated to a higher consciousness, because it demands that we tailor our actions to every individual and each set of circumstances. There is no "one size fits all" philosophy associated with being thoughtful. As the term implies, thoughtfulness requires thought.

Being thoughtful obliges us to consider what others are in need of—from their perspectives, not ours—and mull over what they would most appreciate. It involves deliberately *thinking* about the persons to whom we would like to extend compassion, *determining* through studied calculation what would truly be suitable, and *executing* our ideas even before anyone needs to ask for our assistance. Our actions indicate to the recipients that they were in our thoughts and hearts and that we care enough about them to earnestly reflect on their unique wishes.

There is no "one size fits all" philosophy associated with being thoughtful. As the term implies, thoughtfulness requires thought.

Thoughtfulness is a tangible demonstration of our sensitivity to and regard for others. It is one of the most dynamic elements of engaged compassion because it is not a form of redemption or restitution and has no ulterior motive other than to please or aid the recipient. Thoughtful behavior is the epitome of courtesy, yet it reaches far beyond courtesy's boundaries.

In order to customize thoughtful gestures, we must wield our imaginations and explore what we have to give in light of each situation and the specific needs of the individuals involved. In addition, thoughtfulness involves strategizing and requires a concerted effort to effectively set it in motion. The attention that goes into a single act of thoughtfulness is evident, even if it entails nothing more than fluffing an ill friend's pillow, fetching a glass of water, or offering a backrub. This is perhaps why thoughtfulness is always so deeply appreciated—it is a bona fide gift of the heart.

Acts of thoughtfulness are not measured by their breadth or effect. For someone in need, a hug or a kind word is priceless. What is essential, however, is that the gestures fit the recipient and the occasion and that they are initiated by the giver.

The defining characteristic of thoughtfulness is that it is not solicited. If someone asks us to do something and we follow through with it, we are merely being compliant, not thoughtful. Being thoughtful means that we are interested enough to notice on our own what is needed and that we care enough to take the time and trouble to attend to it.

Courtesy and thoughtfulness go hand in hand. Courtesy is the moon and thoughtfulness the stars. They illuminate the dark recesses of our lives and cheer our spirits. No matter how many times we behold them, they never lose their brilliance, and we never lose our awe. Each beam of courtesy and every twinkle of thoughtfulness steadfastly delight and surprise us time and time again.

ENGAGED LISTENING

We seldom think about our ability to listen because listening is innate, something we do automatically without ever having been taught how to do it. We tend to think of listening as a passive activity. Sounds come into earshot and we hear them without even trying. Consequently, we don't pay much, if any, attention to the *quality* of our listening. We presume that we are proficient merely because we are capable.

The reality is that most of us have dreadful listening skills. Because we tend to be out of touch with the present moment while our minds flit about, we miss a great deal of the words that are spoken to us. Muddling matters further, our daily lives are teeming with random babble from televisions and radios and "white noise," which includes everything from low-voltage electrical buzz to high-speed traffic. We relegate these sounds to the depths of our unconscious, but they don't actually disappear. It may seem that we notice them less and less if we don't deliberately pay them any heed, but they are nevertheless intrusive, adding clutter to our minds, distracting us, and thus preventing us from wholly engaging our attention.

When we want to hear something in particular, we must drown out the din around us so we can zero in on what interests us. In a way, it's like turning down one speaker on our sound systems and turning up another. We can never completely turn off either speaker as long as the system is on and something is playing, but we can muffle certain sounds or make them less audible. Often we may find ourselves tuning in to someone's voice, such as a friend, partner, teacher, or public lecturer, only to absentmindedly tune out, catching just a portion of what was said. Where did our minds go for the rest of the colloquy? What happened to our ears and their ability to hear? Listening doesn't seem so second-nature when we think about how much we normally miss hearing in the course of a day.

Teenagers often joke that their parents can't hear them when they are speaking face to face, but they are amazed at how significantly their parents' hearing improves when they are whispering to a friend in the next room. We all hear what we want to hear. It's what I call "selective hearing loss." Part of the problem with our inability to fully listen is that we have become so adept at habitually shutting out what we *don't* want to hear that we have trouble concentrating on what we *do* want to hear. In addition, our lives are so complex and crowded that our minds are incessantly fixated on what we need to do next, making it hard to just be present and pay attention to what is being said at this very moment.

Whenever people speak, we subliminally weigh whether what they are saying is important to us. If what we want to think about is more interesting or meaningful than the conversation at hand, we'll attend to our thoughts and miss a large portion of what is being said. It's not that we intend to be rude; nonetheless, it's a very bad habit that most of us have adopted. We generally tolerate this idiosyncrasy in ourselves, but it sure is annoying when others do it to *us,* isn't it?

Everyone wants to be heard. We all feel that what we have to say is fascinating, profound, engrossing, or significant, so it's offensive and infuriating when our words are ignored and we have to recapitulate. We have no choice but to believe that the person with whom we are speaking doesn't find us engaging or value what we have to say. It becomes embarrassing, not to mention exhausting, for both the speaker and the listener when what was just said moments earlier has to be rehashed.

Engaged listening is a form of active communication that entails being mindful of and reflecting the thoughts and feelings that are conveyed by another's words. It is not cross-examining, counseling, advising, reprimanding, or a time to retell our own experiences.

Good listening is a talent that is cultivated; it is not instinctive. In addition to wanting to be a conscientious listener, engaged listening takes a concentrated effort. And, as with any other skill, competent listening requires significant practice. It also necessitates following a few basic ground rules.

The Six Principles of Engaged Listening

To be fully engaged in listening, observe the six guidelines that both explain and steer the process. Each guideline is essential, and your success as a listener depends on your ability to employ all six of them deftly and concurrently.

137

1. Keep all diversions at bay.
2. Ignore unrelated thoughts.
3. Reflect what you hear.
4. Acknowledge presence.
5. Wait to exhale.
6. Suspend judgment.

Keep all diversions at bay.
Most of us lead such busy lives that we are always trying to do several things at once, cut corners where we can, and save a little time. Because listening seems so effortless, we try to fit it in with other endeavors, but invariably it receives short shrift. How many times have you tried to cook, use the computer, read the newspaper, or drive while attempting to listen to someone talk? And how many times have you ruined dinner, lost files, reread

articles, or narrowly escaped a potential accident simply because you couldn't devote your complete attention to either activity? Human beings are not designed to work on two tasks simultaneously and do both or either of them proficiently. In spite of our good intentions, something has to give.

In order to listen effectively, devote yourself wholly to it. Not only will you be able to glean more from what you hear, but the other party will know that your attention is not divided. It's not enough to mentally block out distractions; you must physically bar them as well and listen to what is being said as if it is the single most pressing matter in front of you.

138 *Ignore unrelated thoughts.*

To be an expert listener, do not permit your thoughts to yank away your attention. They will no doubt pull at you like a child tugging on a pants leg, but when you are actively listening, all thoughts must be put on hold. Thoughts are merely one more obstacle impeding your ability to remain alert. Still, they can be very seductive. Subdue your thoughts by reminding yourself, "I can think about these concerns later. Right now I am only listening."

Engaged listening is an ideal test of your ability to stay present. In essence, it is an interactive form of meditation. As in meditation, you can bring your wandering mind back to the moment just by being alert to it when it strays. Without criticizing yourself, simply begin listening again as soon as you notice that you have digressed. It may take a fair amount of repetition and discipline before you feel reasonably confident about your proficiency, but the more you do it, the easier and more comfortable it will become.

Reflect what you hear.

Effective listening involves hearing what someone is saying. This seems so simplistic and obvious, but there is much more to being a conscientious listener than acting as a willing receptor. The people who talk to us usually have no idea if we have *accurately* heard what they said. They may assume that we have heard them correctly, but that could be entirely false.

We hear with our minds as well as our ears. Everything that enters our ears is filtered through our minds and hence our worldviews. It is challenging to hear without bias, but this is exactly what engaged listening requires. The only way we can determine if we are listening accurately, and allow speakers a chance to confirm that they were heard reliably and understood, is to reflect back what we think they said. Reflective listening is not parroting precisely what was spoken, which is something no one appreciates hearing, but rather paraphrasing their words and the feelings we perceive are behind them. This will seem strange and awkward at first because it is something we are not accustomed to doing. The more we use this technique, however, the more relaxed and natural it will feel. Even though reflective listening may seem peculiar to you at the onset, it is practically guaranteed to reap positive results if properly employed. We all like to be heard, and reflective listening is the only way to provide that space for others, as well as give them the room to grant it to us. Whether or not there are any outward signs of gratitude, rest assured that your efforts will be greatly welcomed.

Reflective listening does not involve "reading between the lines," interpreting, or analyzing what someone has said. It is simply a straightforward mirroring of what you heard. By putting

139

forth what you believe was said and the emotions you heard the speaker express—without judging them—you will acknowledge that you were listening, and the speaker will have an opportunity to correct you if anything was misheard and help you to get it right.

Keep in mind that reflective listening is not an interrogation. So often when we converse with others we question everything that comes out of their mouths. Reflective listening is the opposite of this tactic. It asks us to hear and then rephrase what we heard in the form of a statement, not a question. In reflective listening, the *only* time a question is appropriate is strictly for clarification, when we truly do not understand what was being said. Other than these infrequent occasions, reflective listening will be framed as a statement.

Here are some examples of how reflective listening should and should not sound.

Example 1:

SPEAKER: I can't believe my boss wants me to work again this weekend. It's as if she thinks I have nothing better to do with my life!

LISTENER:
Assuming: You sure have a horrible boss!
Analyzing: Does she ask anyone else to work on the weekends?
Judging and advising: Don't be so cowardly. Stick up for yourself and tell her off!
Concluding: The problem is that you let everyone push you around.
Condemning: You should at least be grateful that you have a job!

Minimizing: Working weekends isn't such a big issue. Lots of people have to work weekends.

Negating: So what else do you have to do instead that's so important? Just go to work and stop complaining about it.

Engaged: You feel your boss is regularly taking advantage of you and doesn't respect your free time.

Example 2:

SPEAKER: I've been to five doctors in the past six months, but no one can seem to figure out what's wrong with me!

LISTENER:

Assuming: I know what you mean. The medical profession stinks!

Analyzing: What are your symptoms?

Judging: You're such a worry wart!

Advising: I use a great alternative practitioner you might be interested in.

Concluding: You need to be more assertive if you want to get some answers.

Minimizing: Just put it out of your mind. There are a lot of people who are much worse off than you are.

Negating: Did you ever think that maybe it's all in your head?

Engaged: On top of being ill, you're feeling extremely frustrated and disappointed.

Example 3:

SPEAKER: You better get this report done immediately. You know this is our biggest client!

LISTENER:

Assuming: This client is always making unreasonable demands.

Analyzing: Why are you so anxious about this?
Judging and deflecting: You sure are crabby today. What's really the matter?
Reprimanding: Stop pressuring me!
Self-directing: I've got other work I need to get done first.
Minimizing: It's not all that important. I'll get it done eventually.
Negating: Simmer down. You're getting yourself all worked up over nothing.
Engaged: This report is very important, and it needs to be completed as soon as possible.

Example 4:

SPEAKER: My wife is having an affair and wants to leave me. I love her, but what can I do?

LISTENER:
Assuming: She's always had a wandering eye.
Analyzing: How do you know she's running around on you?
Advising and judging: You could have an affair of your own. That would serve her right!
Judging: She's a creep. I don't see any point in sticking around.
Advising: Maybe a marriage counselor could help.
Concluding: You just need to be more of a man and lay down the law.
Minimizing: Lots of couples have affairs. I don't see what the big deal is.
Negating: It's just one little dalliance. Forget about it.
Engaged: This is heartbreaking for you. You don't want your marriage to end, but you don't know what your options are.

Remember, an engaged listener's responses are presented as statements, not questions, so your vocal intonation should remain even or be lowered at the end of each sentence. However, it should never rise at the end, as with a question. This is critical, because questions and an inquiring tone put people on the defensive. They make us feel as if our emotions and thoughts are being doubted rather than plainly accepted as our personal truths. As an engaged listener, it is your responsibility to let speakers know that you are hearing what they tell you, not quizzing them, being sarcastic, telling them what to do, judging or downplaying their feelings, jumping to conclusions, or examining the accuracy of what they say.

If speakers feel an engaged listener has misconstrued what they said, they will edit what the listener reflected to them. For example:

143

.☙

> SPEAKER: I feel that I do everything around the house and never get any help.
>
> ENGAGED LISTENER: The burden of housekeeping is totally on your shoulders.
>
> SPEAKER: Well, yes, I do the majority of the work. But I must admit that my partner helps out a lot. It's just that the kids never want to do their share.

In this instance, the speaker was able to clarify that the problem was with his children rather than his partner. Here's another example taken a little farther:

> SPEAKER: Every time we go out to dinner we end up going to the restaurants you select.
>
> ENGAGED LISTENER: You feel that I don't take your preferences into consideration when we go out to eat.
>
> SPEAKER: I must admit that I always enjoy where we go, and I know you're aware of what I like, but I wish we'd try out some of my ideas now and then, too.

ENGAGED LISTENER: You'd like to have an equal say in where we go.

SPEAKER: You bet!

ENGAGED LISTENER: Okay, that's fine with me. Do you have any suggestions for our next dinner outing?

Reflective listening can and should evolve into conversation—a give and take between talking and listening—otherwise it becomes stale and irritating. Certainly there will be times when listening is all that is germane, such as consoling a troubled friend, but most often we want our interactions to be interactive. Nevertheless, reflective listening is an invaluable talent that will add depth to any relationship and make every dialogue more meaningful. It is also a vital link in the chain of compassion because we cannot extend ourselves effectively if we are unable to clearly hear what someone is candidly telling us.

Acknowledge presence.

Have you ever had conversations with people who you were certain didn't hear a word you said? They may not have been distracted by anything conspicuous; maybe they were just looking out the window, down at the floor, up at the ceiling, or had their head completely turned away from you. Perhaps they were tapping their fingers on the table or they mumbled a superficial "mmhm" when they caught a momentary pause. Whatever minor notice they thought they were giving you became pointless and humiliating. They knew they weren't listening to you, but they thought they could fool you all the same. You knew they weren't listening to you, but you felt obliged to pretend they were. What silly games we sometimes play!

Face-to-face communications necessitate eye contact—not staring, but genuinely looking at the other person—if your interest is to be believed. (Note that in some cultures eye contact is considered a sign of disrespect, not regard. Thus it may be necessary to tailor this or other behaviors to the customs of the people with whom you are interacting.) To demonstrate compassion as you listen, pay attention, remain relaxed and open, and behave as though nothing else matters to you at this moment except what the speakers are saying and feeling. This acknowledges their presence, affirms their worth, and lets them know that your attention is focused squarely on them and nowhere else.

Sometimes nonsexual touching, such as a friendly hug or a hand on the shoulder or forearm, lets other people know you care about them, without having to speak a word. Again, bear in mind that some cultures and religions find this offensive, especially between people of the opposite sex. Be sensitive to this, particularly if the person speaking is someone you do not know well. Although touch can be very comforting, some people interpret it as a power play, not just between the sexes but among people of different ages, income levels, ethnic groups, job positions, and other hierarchical associations, so be aware of this as well.

In addition to nonverbally confirming that you are conscious of the speaker, you need to signal your own presence, too. So often we think of listening as being dull and dormant, as though a stuffed doll could do an equally competent job. But nobody wants to talk to dead weight. We long for a living, breathing, responsive person at the other end of our words. On rare occasions there may not be appropriate moments to interject reflective listening; still, if you say nothing at all, it will seem

145

as though your body is there but your mind is not. In this case, an intermittent "I see," or "Oh my," or "How wonderful," or some other brief but appropriate comment inserted at the proper times will be more sensible. This is always true, of course, for telephone conversations, where any nonverbal communication is perfectly useless.

Wait to exhale.

Although we are hardly ever conscious of it, most of us spend the time we should be listening anticipating our chances to speak. Our minds are ruminating about a clever idea or comment or we can't wait to share something about our own experiences. Listening is not a test of our ability to wait for a good opening. It is also not the time to be contemplating the ingenious remarks we want to make. If we are doing either one of these, we are not fully listening. In fact, we are probably not listening at all, but focusing on ourselves and our own needs or sense of self-importance.

In every conversation, the people speaking need to be allowed to finish what they began. They need to get out their thoughts completely, without us finishing their sentences for them or cutting them off. Otherwise they will lose their flow and spend the rest of the conversation trying to remember what it is they forgot. They also will feel insulted if they are interrupted midstream, as if what they are saying is less important than what the interrupter has to say. Moreover, if we let people complete what they have to say, we can better understand what they want to express, instead of trying to second-guess them.

Engaged conversations go back and forth between active speaking and active listening. But there should always be a momentary lull between either role. When other people have finished speaking, count slowly to three before responding. Let there be enough space between their final word and your first one to digest what was said and provide an opening for them to add more, if they so choose. Those three slow seconds are short enough not to be strained and long enough to give you time to collect your thoughts and take a deep breath before you speak.

Suspend judgment.
Hearing without evaluating is perhaps the most demanding aspect of engaged listening. Yet being critiqued for what we say is not what anybody desires. We just want to be heard, not analyzed, and certainly not judged. Even so, we are often quick to give our opinions when people share their feelings and experiences with us, despite the fact that we wouldn't ever wish this for ourselves.

When we express our unsolicited viewpoints of others' situations, we imply that they are too dense to see matters clearly, or they don't have the insights that we do. We also presume that they haven't thoroughly thought through their options, and the only reason they are telling us these things is that they want our advice. The truth is that they don't want our advice. If they did, they would ask for it outright. It's aggravating and demeaning when suggestions are dumped on us as if we don't have a clue about our circumstances or the vaguest idea how to solve our problems. When other people start grilling us or freely express their opinions of how we are handling our lives, we are made to feel stupid, inadequate, or out of control.

It is arrogant to assume that we know more than others do about how they should live their lives. We may believe we do,

147

but, in reality, this can never be the case. We cannot ever fully know or have access to the histories, emotions, relationships, and experiences that merge to make others who they are, so we couldn't possibly understand what would be best for them. It makes no difference if the people we are dealing with are our parents, children, colleagues, friends, or life mates; none of us wants to be judged.

Foisting unwanted opinions and advice on others robs them of their autonomy and self-respect. When we listen, we need to just listen—not counsel, suggest, or evaluate. It is not as easy as it sounds, but since engaged listening is perhaps the freest and most generous gift of compassion that we can offer, it is well worth the study time. Engaged listening is a talent and skill unto itself, and despite all outward appearances, it has nothing to do with the health of our hearing and everything to do with the openness of our hearts.

SILENCE

It may seem that silence and engaged listening are two sides of the same coin, but, in fact, they have very little in common. The quick lull between listening and speaking is the only time that listening and silence graze shoulders. Silence is a period when *all* forms of communication—speaking *and* listening—are deliberately suspended. Overall, silence has more in common with meditation than with listening, especially if we postpone our inner dialogues as well.

Our hectic lives give us hardly any chance to escape communication. Discourse constantly chases us in one form or another, and it's not only person-to-person exchanges that harry us. Listening, reading, writing, using the computer, and even thinking and daydreaming are all forms of communication, one-sided though they may seem. In the bustle of our culture, people feel the pressure to fill in every gap with some sort of stimulation. As a whole, we are uncomfortable with silent moments, so we do everything we can to avoid them by not letting a second go by without some chatter in it. We feel that one-on-one interactions must be brimming with talk no less than business meetings or social gatherings. Breakfast calls for the weather report, a simple walk or a short drive demands music, and many people can't get through their evening meals without the accompaniment of the nightly news. Is there any way that we can sidestep this ceaseless commotion that rattles our nerves, upsets our stomachs, and unsettles our dispositions?

149

> It is as important for our minds and spirits to have silence as it is for our bodies to have rest and repose.

Silence gives us a break from communicating and offers our minds a breather in much the same way that meditation does, except that silence is less structured. As long as we calm our thoughts simultaneously, silence can take the shape of painting or sculpting, weaving or crocheting, cooking, cleaning, or walking in the woods. Silence is chameleonlike, so it can be created whenever and however we choose, assuming we are surrounded by quiet and solitude or people who respect our wishes.

It is as important for our minds and spirits to have silence as it is for our bodies to have rest and repose. Thus, strive each day to make room for silence, whether it is during your drive to the office, mealtime, exercise time, yoga practice, or while working in the garden. The same techniques used in meditation apply to your silent times. Focus on what you are doing or on your breath and simply let your thoughts drift by without attaching yourself to them. Your practice of silence can range from ten minutes to several hours, or it may fluctuate in length from day to day depending on your schedule and commitments. Regardless of how busy our lives may seem, if we make time for silence we will feel refreshed, relaxed, and more capable of concentrating on all the tasks we have at hand, including our compassion.

Silence gently reminds us to keep the knowledge of our good deeds to ourselves. An amazing energy is stoked when we don't discuss our acts of compassion. Staying silent about them safeguards us from investing ego and pride in our benevolent endeavors, and it shields recipients from any potential embarrassment they may experience from such disclosures. For the most part, we are the only ones who need to know about them, so other than for vanity, there is rarely a compelling reason to tell anyone else. There is a joyful, private pleasure in keeping our charitable acts secret.

Silence also refers to knowing when to "hold your tongue" so you don't engage in hurtful or distracting pastimes such as gossiping, bragging, slander, or idle small talk. When you are comfortable with silence, you can call on it at any time to prevent sticking your foot in your mouth or saying something you will later regret. If you get into a sticky situation, first invoke the gift of silence. Remember it, and it will always be available to assist you. Indeed, there are times when saying nothing speaks volumes more than saying anything at all.

HUMOR

People who engage their compassion and thoroughly integrate it into their lives may find that they are readily susceptible to heartaches and depression about the world's seemingly endless ills and our limited abilities to invoke reforms. Opening up and exposing our hearts keeps us soft and tender, but it makes us vulnerable, too. Despite the good that we are doing, we can easily become frustrated and morose. Sadness can paralyze us and prevent us from being the instruments of loving-kindness that we truly are. Learning to see the positive sides of life, which always exist regardless of how many dark clouds obstruct our view, not only will help us be more productive and caring, it will make us more peaceful and whole human beings.

151

> Humor is food for the spirit, and without it we are malnourished.

Laughter is the best tonic no matter what the malady. It helps to heal us on every level and makes the anguish we face more bearable. Although the issues that many of us deal with may be very serious, humor helps ease our loads, keeps our spirits light, prevents burnout, and affirms that life is worth living. Sobering activities can be draining, but laughter refuels our verve. It is not a frivolous diversion. Humor is food for the spirit, and without it we are malnourished.

There are different kinds of humor, but not all of them are healthful. Learning to laugh at ourselves and the inadequacies that are simply part of the human condition is among the best humor. It relieves us of our heavy sense of self-importance and reminds us of our membership in the community of life. It also helps us to be less solemn about our mistakes and know that our flub-ups, big or small, are shared by others and are not the end of the world.

Laughing *with* others as they laugh at themselves and finding humor in the ironies of living are also healing. But laughing *at* others, belittling them, or demeaning them or the groups with which they are affiliated is not funny; it is offensive. No matter if the people we are laughing at are present or not, this type of humor is a put-down, plain and simple. Whether it's racist, homo- or hetero-sexist, classist, religious, or ethnic in content, if we find amusement in stereotyping or maligning others, we shame and belittle ourselves and those we coax into joining us.

Whenever you feel down or sluggish, the first remedy to reach for is a large dose of restorative laughter. Before you give up or cave in, look for something humorous in your situation or your behavior that you might have overlooked, talk to a friend who knows how to make you laugh, read an amusing book, or watch a comedy. Loosen up and let yourself roar at a good joke; it is an amazing release. Seek out events or people that make you smile, chuckle, or laugh out loud. Indulge yourself if someone inserts an irreverent dash of humor into an otherwise sedate discussion, or take the initiative if you are so inclined.

Humor does not detract from engaged compassion; rather, it enhances it. It makes our communications richer and more enjoyable. It initiates beaming smiles. It delights our minds, buoys our spirits, and brings joy to those who see our happy faces. Certainly humor is not the cake of compassion, but it is definitely the icing. Humor makes the cake more tempting and beautiful and the taste even more pleasing and sweet.

10

The Portal
of Serenity

A feeling of inner calm and peacefulness is the natural consequence of engaged compassion. In addition, serenity may be intentionally developed in conjunction with engaged compassion in order to accentuate the tranquil demeanor that precedes and fosters benevolent action. Our frenetic society promotes agitation, which can lead to unrest, moodiness, and stormy conduct. Maintaining serenity can help us weather tough times and maneuver through an often chaotic culture while staying centered and keeping our ethical perspectives intact.

Being competent at serenity takes dedicated practice; it is not an accident of nature. It also must be made a priority if you want to master it successfully and have it become a spontaneous part of your repertoire. The portal of serenity can be navigated concurrently with any of the other gateways. It teaches us that our inner realms are inherently tethered to our outward behaviors. Who we are determines how we will act; therefore, how we act is a reflection of who we are.

PATIENCE

Although patience is an anomaly these days, it is no less a virtue than it was a hundred or more years ago. Furthermore, our abilities to develop patience have not diminished from lack of use. We are just as capable as ever of being patient, but because we have become accustomed to an abnormally accelerated pace of technology, travel, and communication, we are in need of it more fervently than at almost any other time in history.

Patience pertains to our competence at slowing down, not rushing our decisions, our work, our meals, our play, our lives. Learning to live in the moment helps us to be more patient, as does daily meditation. When we are anxious for events to transpire, we completely miss what we are experiencing right now because we are concentrating on what we anticipate will unfold.

We could best define patience as an ability to wait without getting flustered. Usually we become irritated about the slow pace of circumstances, because we believe that what we expect to happen is more important than what is happening while we wait. We forget that life doesn't respond to our wishes or stop occurring just because we want it to move faster. Cogitating how our time could be spent more productively than merely by "waiting" incites us to anger and indignation. Tapping our toes or fingers, pacing, and shaking our heads only rile us up further. The time that we could have spent calming ourselves and practicing self-control and perseverance is frittered away feeding our egos—How could they do this to me? Don't they know I have better things to do than wait around all day?—and stirring up frantic emotions.

> If we expect the world to move to our rhythms, we must accept that others will be out of step.

Everyone moves at a velocity that feels comfortable, but one person's run is another person's crawl. If we expect the world to move to our rhythms, we must accept that others will be out of step. There is no single rate that suits everyone equally. In the final analysis, it may not be "they" who are out of stride, but us. Therefore, to avoid the exasperation that comes with demanding an impossible conformity to our notion of "right speed," we must abandon the idea altogether.

The easiest way to save ourselves the frustration of impatience is to adapt as best as possible to other people's speed zones instead of expecting them to accommodate ours. We cannot force others to move more quickly or slowly, but we can restrain the demands we place on them, letting them and ourselves off the hook simultaneously.

When you find yourself getting antsy, stop and notice where the feeling is coming from and where it is manifesting in your body. Think about what is precipitating the feeling and acknowledge that you are living right now, not in some more agreeable time in the near future. Pay attention to how you are

157

breathing—simply notice your breath, the length and depth of each inhalation and exhalation, as well the pauses in between. Be aware of the tension in your body, starting from the top of your head and working your way down through each muscle and limb. When you discover an area that is taut and strained, think "relax, relax." See if you can pinpoint exactly where the tension is located and where it begins and ends. Give each tense spot your fullest attention before moving on to the next part of your body. As you wholly attend to the tension in your body and gently ask it to relax, you will notice it melt away, without any force or extra effort. As you exhale, imagine the released tension flowing down through your body, out through your feet and toes, and into the earth where it will be purified and purged.

158

Observing your breath and tension will automatically bring you back to the moment at hand. It dissipates the anxiety of not getting our way with the timing of the world and soothes the edginess that comes with feeling out of control.

When we fret over lost time, we lose more than just the time we have at the moment. There is a recovery period afterward when we attempt to regain the equilibrium lost during a self-induced bout of "stressitis." The amount of time involved in being ticked off and regrouping is usually far greater than the time we worry about having lost. For instance, if people are late for an appointment with you and you are left stewing for fifteen minutes, and you stay annoyed for another fifteen or thirty minutes after they arrive or leave, what good has it done you? In what way is being impatient constructive? Will your annoyance speed them up, make your day more pleasant or fruitful, or do anything to inspire contentment in yourself and those around you?

Rarely is restlessness self-contained. When we are itchy and agitated, we aggravate everyone around us. It doesn't change our situation or hurry anyone else along; it just makes everybody uneasy. In the end, what was the rush all about? Speeding through life only increases the proximity of our death. There is nothing to hurry toward. Will being flustered over a few lost minutes today truly matter a year from now? Five years from now? Ten years from now? Of course not. But the effects we have on those around us could influence them long after we recuperate from our own self-inflicted intolerance.

Patience is the glow of serenity. If others try to undermine yours, breathe deeply, hold fast, and realize that if you remain serene, you will accomplish more in the same amount of time than those who succumb to the pressures of a phantom finish line. When we are patient, we have all the time in the world to savor each morsel of life and to fully perceive every precious experience. We bring a sense of peacefulness to all that we do, and beyond simply talking about tranquility, we learn how to actually live it.

159

COMPOSURE

Ernest Hemingway said, "Courage is grace under pressure," and indeed this holds much wisdom. To remain poised in oppressive situations requires self-control and balance, two essential components of composure. When we become perturbed or irate, which are opposites of being composed, we allow matters to get to us, to burrow under our skin and stay there. In order to be bothered, our pride and egos must grab center stage. They are what cause us to take things personally, lose our composure, and get angry.

The ego is a magnet for what we perceive to be personal injustices. If we believe we have been wronged, ego steps in to protect us. Unfortunately, ego is a provocateur and not a good choice to help maintain the peace. Our egos are like sticky paper: rage, resentment, hostility, and envy bond to them like glue. We can tell that ego is involved when we have thoughts that begin with, "How dare she," or "What gives him the right," or "Who does he think he is," or "She doesn't know whom she's dealing with," or any similar notion that obliterates the worth of others while elevating our own sense of importance. As long as we allow ego to rule our responses and behavior, composure will remain a stranger.

We have been conditioned to believe that we must fight fire with fire. But all that gets us is a bigger fire. Instead of building blazes or fanning flames, there are two helpful methods for dealing with situations when composure seems out of reach.

Walk Away

No disagreeable circumstance requires a split-second decision, which is almost guaranteed to get us into trouble. Instead of reacting, we can literally extricate ourselves—physically or mentally—from almost any potential conflict. Beyond the pull of ego, there is nothing that compels us to respond to any non-bodily assault—now or ever—no matter how offensive it may be. If you are unable to exit the room, walk away mentally just by not responding. If a rejoinder seems mandatory, smile, take a few slow, deep breaths, and diplomatically state, "I do not engage in confrontations," "This subject is not open for discussion," "I do not want to get into a debate," or any other comment that will defuse the situation and make your point.

It takes two to argue. If one party is unwilling to participate, the sparks will be extinguished. Maintaining composure basically entails not letting our egos run the show and walk all over us and everybody else. If we respond out of anger, even for just a brief moment—and that's all it will amount to—we may think we are getting the upper hand, venting our emotions, or defending ourselves. In the end, however, when we lose our composure, we lose control over both the situation and ourselves.

161

> We have been conditioned to believe that we must fight fire with fire. But all that gets us is a bigger fire.

When the opportunity exists to postpone a response, take advantage of it. With a delay, you can walk away for minutes, hours, days, weeks, or whatever the time frame permits. Once your mind is disengaged from a direct threat, you'll be able to think more clearly and rationally. Then, when you do respond, you can do so while staying calm and collected. Time is a splendid leveler. The more time you can gain for yourself when facing a possible confrontation, the better chance you'll have of keeping your composure intact and the greater likelihood that all parties will emerge unscathed.

Nonownership

We are not obliged to catch or hold on to what others toss our way. If we refuse ownership of other people's negative comments and barbs, they will have no power over us.

Two mental images can help you retain your composure and thwart your ego before it seizes command. One is to imagine that your body is lacquered with a smooth, very slippery, nonstick coating. Absolutely nothing can stick to you. Then envision that every derogatory statement, hurtful remark, or cruel encounter just slides off you and into the ground below or the atmosphere around you to be purified and dissolved. Alternatively, picture yourself made of pure, transparent light, a light so brilliant it is white or golden with shimmering rays around the edges. Visualize painful words, attitudes, and situations traveling right through your luminous self, unable to take hold. Touching your light they are rendered powerless and benign.

Concentrate on your breathing as you focus on your mental image. Just observe each inhalation and exhalation as you watch the pain slide off or through you and made completely harmless.

Another technique for maintaining your cool is to observe your physical reactions to tense situations. Our bodies indicate what we are feeling inside, generally long before we are even aware of the emotions that are flooding us. Notice when the tenor of your body shifts. Try to distinguish the areas where you start to get tight—your face, lips, jaw, throat, back of the neck, shoulders, legs, hands, or elsewhere. Pay attention to the rate and depth of your breathing. Is it constricted, shallow, or quick? Is your heart racing? Are your temples pounding? Are your ears flushed and hot? Do you get tics or engage in nervous habits?

See if you can detect all the ways your body responds when you are feeling piqued, troubled, or threatened. Studying our reactions is not only instructive, it also helps to ground us, center us, and bring our attention back to the moment where our composure patiently awaits us.

Frequently anger is precipitated by assumptions and misinformation. We often don't have the full story, but we jump to conclusions anyway, based solely on conjecture. It's not uncommon to find out later that our theories pulled us and our emotions in a completely erroneous direction, and we got all puffed up over nothing. Many times there is another side, or several other sides, to the situation, or an important piece of information that we overlooked or didn't have.

As soon as you recognize the symptoms of your vanishing composure, remind yourself that you are taking matters personally, that you are letting someone else's viewpoint manipulate and usurp your own, and what you see is probably not all there is to know. Next, acknowledge the role that your ego is playing in trying to throw you off course. Then, finally, implement the strategies of "walk away" and "nonownership" to regain your composure and perspective.

Fortunately, these simple approaches can help us whenever our grace starts to crumble and we teeter off kilter, and they are always right at our fingertips. It is only when we cling to harsh assertions and let our egos respond that we lose our balance. When we learn how to let go of hurt before it harms us by not even letting it enter our minds and spirits, let alone lodge in our bodies, we will understand how to master the art of composure, and we will be able to retain our peaceful centers no matter in what circumstances we find ourselves.

WONDER

Children are naturally filled with awe about the world around them. They tend to accept that this life is packed with miracles, and they marvel at its splendor. As we grow older, we are taught to question, investigate, and dissect the mysteries that surround us, and, like a magic trick revealed, the wonders of childhood unravel.

Being amazed at the natural world and enamored with life are gifts that are not relegated solely to the young and innocent. We adults can regain those feelings of wonder by taking time to contemplate and meditate on the spectacles of existence. For example:

- Where does the wind begin?
- What causes seeds to sprout?
- How does a flower know when to bloom?
- Where do our thoughts come from?
- Why does everything that is living age and die?
- Where were we before we were born?
- Are our emotions real or imagined?
- Where does the sky end?

Pondering the secrets of life keeps us intrigued and mesmerized as adults. There is no need to reason away life's mysteries, as doing so only detracts from our delight. Embracing wonder means allowing the unknown to endure without slaying its magic through the indignities of scientific inquiry and analysis. We don't need to have a technical explanation for everything we encounter. We can let the world and our wonder just abide.

Wonder makes us feel large and small simultaneously. It fills our hearts and spirits with exhilaration and lets us experience once again the surprises of our youth. Wonder is a state of curiosity and astonishment that liberates the eternal children within us. It humbles us and keeps us connected to the marvels that affect and are a part of all life.

Your sense of wonder affirms your conscious awareness and lets you know that you are fully alive. When we lose our awe we become hardened, stony, and incapable of feeling. A detached, analytical mind is impervious and unemotional. Without sensitivity, we lose the capacity to empathize, and thus we forfeit our abilities to be compassionate.

Right outside our windows and deep inside our hearts there are countless opportunities to engage our wonder. Select one, two, or three wondrous gifts to think about and be thankful for every day. You can use these as part of a wakeful exercise, quiet meditation, or appreciative prayer. Our proficiency at being impressed by the natural world is a gauge of our openness and accessibility. Let your wonder flourish and grow.

UNITY

There are many ways to define *unity,* but in the context of engaged compassion it refers to the interconnectedness of all life. If you imagine a large umbrella with every living being gathered underneath, you will have a picture of what unity looks like. Engaged compassion asks us to stand under this umbrella, to look around and realize that all people, all other animals, and the earth and plants that sustain us are part of one family—the family of life—and that no amount of pretense can obscure this fact.

On a visceral level we know that the life force in us is no different than that within any other sentient living being. When we dig down deep enough, to the point of total honesty, we discover that neither euphemisms nor camouflage can erase this fundamental piece of knowledge from the core of our awareness. Our fellowship with life is what makes us humane; without it we are barely human.

Only when we find peace in our hearts through love and camaraderie toward all life will our incessant human-to-human and interspecies holocausts cease. There can be no hierarchy of human superiority, for it is this very arrogance that has mired our world in discord and combat. Each living entity has its peerless capabilities, so it is irrelevant who is better at what. Excellence, mediocrity, and inferiority do not make any of us more or less worthy than another. We are all leaves on the same tree. Petals on the same flower. Clouds in the same sky. Without any one of us the world would be diminished and imbalanced.

What we don't understand is no less important than what we do understand. The unknown is crucial, if only for the very reason that we do not know what truths it holds. Speculation about what we *want* to believe, versus what is genuinely true or unknown, has caused us to abandon unity to chase after our desires. When we face our sisters and brothers, when we look into their eyes, we cannot deny that we are cut from the same cloth, molded from the same clay. There is a drop within each of us that is part of a single ocean of life. The primary differences among us concern our packaging, not our substance.

Living with a conscious appreciation of unity brings us peace of mind, heart, and spirit. It is a natural outcome of wholly engaged compassion, as well as an impetus to activate our benevolence more completely. Without espousing unity, our efforts in

166

the realm of compassion will be hopelessly compromised and fragmented. However, when we incorporate unity into our worldviews, we find an expanded, loving family and a neighborhood of braided spirits that spans the globe.

CONTENTMENT

Contentment is nothing more than being satisfied with who we are, where we are, and with what we have right now. Each of our lives is a tapestry of moments, with each moment a separate stitch. When we study an individual stitch, we can see that it is perfect. It doesn't matter if it is shorter or longer than any other, or crooked or even. When we do not compare one stitch to another, we find each to be flawless and functional, the impeccable outcome of the stitch before it and precisely what is necessary to support the one that follows.

Within the moments of our lives—the stitches of our tapestries—there is contentment. There is no longing to be elsewhere or someone other than who we are. When we are fully present in *this* moment we are not looking to the future or brooding about the past. We are here, and here is the only place where contentment can be found.

> Each of our lives is a tapestry of moments, with each moment a separate stitch. Here in *this* moment is the only place where contentment can be found.

167

New clothes, more money, a bigger car, the consummate partner are window dressing, not the real thing. When our compassion is wholly engaged, we realize this intuitively. Our passions and desires do not exist in this moment but rather in the moments we anticipate and for which we hunger. Right now, however, there is serenity. Right now we possess the centering balance we need. Here in this moment is all that we have been, all that we are, and all that we will ever become. This moment contains everything that we can ever truly have or be assured of knowing. Within this very moment lies contentment.

If we are not content within ourselves, we will be unable to give to others in the spirit of engaged compassion. We will be too desperate, wanting, and self-focused. Yet in this moment— despite whatever we may crave or think we lack—we have all that we need. We can even tolerate pain and heartache moment to moment, because in each moment there is wholeness and relief.

As we change our worldviews, our lifestyles, and our habits to engage our compassion to its fullest, we will discover strategies and techniques that encourage and nourish contentment. The peace we develop within ourselves is what we have to extend outward. Thus contentment is vital to engaged compassion and engaged compassion is key to our contentment.

CONCLUSION

As human beings, compassion is our birthright. We were given all the tools, skills, and knowledge we need to engage this defining aspect of our nature. Sadly, our culture has relegated compassion to a rank of low importance, causing us to lose our way, forsake our heritage, and forfeit our membership in the broader family of life. Still, the legacy of loving-kindness lives on inside us; it is eternally etched in the human spirit. Even though it has been buried under a mountain of materialism and the angst of modern living, it is ours to rediscover and reclaim.

Our culture's priorities, tastes, and values are constantly metamorphosing. Although it may seem that powers outside of ourselves dictate these shifting tides, we all play a vital role in determining the course of our shared future. Each year we are subject to new fads, fashions, flavors, and experiences that are either "in" or "out." Although advertising campaigns and other marketing ploys play a significant part in influencing our buying habits, ultimately it is up to the masses to accept or reject new concepts.

There have been plenty of ill-conceived ideas that fell flat because of public disapproval. Yet if enough people concur, a notion can take hold and become enmeshed in our collective psyches. This is the theory of *critical mass,* the premise that when a sufficient number of individuals embrace a new outlook, belief, or practice, it becomes readily assimilated by the majority. We don't know what that exact number is, however, because for every instance it is unique. How many people had to use the word "cool" before it became cool to use it in our casual lingo? How many people needed to access the Internet before it became a necessity? How many people must endorse a particular cuisine to make it the latest rage? The popularity of styles, words, customs, and virtually all our cultural assertions are affected by critical mass more than any other factor.

Because we do not know how many people it would take to establish compassionate living as a cultural standard, each one of us is vitally significant. Will it take one million people, ten million, one hundred million, or more before engaged compassion takes root? You might very well be that crucial individual who puts the numbers over the top!

Positive and lasting cultural change will not evolve through intellectual exercises because core values are never transformed by data. Compassion is an affair of the heart. Therefore, only through entreating the heart and our inner wisdom can we instill the changes we wish to see for ourselves and for the world.

170

There are many ways of looking at compassion. People who are involved with peace, diversity, and social justice issues view compassion in terms of the human condition. Animal rights activists consider compassion with regard to the plight of animals. Environmentalists see compassion in relation to the natural world or the built environment. We have compartmentalized our compassion, channeled and dichotomized it.

Your vibrant example of engaged compassion can help reunite the scattered pieces of this puzzle. Through mindful awareness and acts of loving-kindness, you can spread the understanding that compassion is more than passive caring or concern for favored factions. Rather, it is the everyday practice of true inclusion and the resolute path to healing, wholeness, and harmony.

Start—and continue.

Joanne Stepaniak conducts lectures and workshops on engaged compassion throughout North America. If you would like to arrange a presentation for your group, business, or organization, please write to her at P.O. Box 82663, Swissvale, Pennsylvania 15218, or e-mail her at joanne@compassionatelives.com.

INDEX

A

acceptance
    engaged compassion and, 77,
        85-92
    forgiveness and, 92
    self-acceptance and, 90
acknowledging presence, in
        communications, 144-146
activated compassion. *See*
        engaged compassion
adversity, engaged compassion
        through, 43-44
altruism, 13-14
anger, dealing with, 159-161,
        162-163
animals, engaged compassion
        for, 69-72
antisocial behavior, 12
apathy, overcoming, 75-76
arrogance, 96, 97

attitudes
    actions and, 3, 21
    selflessness and, 99
    smile exercise and, 23-25
awareness, mindful. *See* mindful
        awareness

B

balance
    between narcissism and
        asceticism, 44-46
    worldviews and, 44
beliefs, and cultural blinders. *See*
        worldviews
beneficiaries of kindness, 19, 21
blaming others, 95
branches of compassion, 47-74
breathing, attention to, 29-30,
        114, 116, 162